PERUSALS INTO (POST) MODERN THOUGHT

Claudia Moscovici

University Press of America,® Inc.
Lanham • New York • Oxford

Copyright 2000 by
University Press of America, ® Inc.
4720 Boston Way
Lanham, Maryland 20706

12 Hid's Copse Rd.
Cumnor Hill, Oxford OX2 9JJ

Library of Congress Cataloging-in-Publication Data

Moscovici, Claudia.
Perusals into (post) modern thought / Claudia Moscovici.
p.   cm.
Includes bibliographical references.
1. Postmodernism.   I. Title: Perusals into postmodern thought. II. Title.
B831.2.M68   2000   149'.97—dc21   99-088671 CIP

ISBN 0-7618-1615-1 (cloth: alk. ppr.)

♾™ The paper used in this publication meets the minimum
requirements of American National Standard for Information
Sciences—Permanence of Paper for Printed Library Materials,
ANSI Z39.48—1984

Contents

Part One

Introduction   1

Chapter One   15

    Beyond the universal and the particular

Chapter Two   47
    The postmodern need for a philosophy of
    common sense

Part Two: 69

    Hidden glances,
    silent whispers (novella)

Introduction

Following Jean-François Lyotard's publication of *The Postmodern Condition: A Report on Knowledge,*[1] the term "postmodernism" acquired cultural currency in the United States and France. Although the word originally described the aesthetic innovations of a small group of New York artists in the 1960's, we now find it applied to just about everything, ranging from the dissimulation of politicians regarding their sexual encounters, to beer commercials, to Goddard's movies. At the same time that this term appears everywhere, it also seems to explain nothing. Postmodern critics underscore the sublime elusiveness of the term, pointing to its essential indefinability.[2] The pervasiveness of "postmodernism," however, has also given wake to a more pragmatic approach. Numerous textbooks that introduce students to literary and cultural theory have attempted to curb the seemingly aimless dissemination of the term by defining it more precisely in relation to closely related concepts, including modernism, the avant-garde, poststructuralism, and cultural relativism.[3]

By all accounts--whether one reads the works of postmodern critics such as Jean-François Lyotard, Frederic Jameson, Jean Baudrillard, Zygmunt Bauman or introductions to their works--"postmodernism" represents a complex cultural phenomenon that acquires different meanings in different contexts. Postmodernism signifies a historical and political category that identifies the major transformations of modern capitalist society; a philosophical reaction to Enlightenment thought; or an aesthetic movement that both perpetuates and challenges the innovations of modernism. Before explaining how this book introduces readers to postmodernism in a different manner from other texts on the subject, let me offer some general background to postmodernism and related terms.

a) Postmodernism, modernism and the avant-garde

The modernist and postmodernist movements, as their etymology implies, are closely related. The term modernism generally refers to the art and literature produced from the 1920's to the middle 1950's. It includes movements such as absurdism and symbolism in literature, cubism, futurism, abstract expressionism in the plastic arts, and atonal composition in music, all of which sought to break with the realist traditions established during the nineteenth century. The poetry of Eliot and Pound; the novels of Joyce and Woolf; the paintings of Picasso and Dali; the music of Shoenberg and Berg are all considered to be representative of modern art. Such art rejects the basic premise of nineteenth-century realism, which posits that the purpose of art is to reflect and perhaps change a coherent reality. Emerging between the two world wars, modernist art suggests that neither the human subject nor the world he inhabits is unified and coherent. Viewed through the prism of modernist art, reality consists of a series of fragmentary, incoherent and often violent events that splinter the mastery of the human subject over himself and the world. In its artistic assumptions, modernism includes the more specific movement of the avant-garde. During the mid-1920's to the late 1930's, groups of artists--including surrealists and expressionists--proclaimed that they led the modernist movement, much as the avant-garde leads an army. As Susan Suleiman explains in *Subversive Intent*, "The hallmark of these movements was a collective project . . . that linked artistic experimentation and a critique of outmoded artistic practices with an ideological critique of bourgeois thought and a desire for social change, so that the activity of writing would also be seen as a genuine intervention in the social, cultural and political arena."[4]

Although postmodern artists such as Andy Warhol and Jackson Pollock and filmmakers such as Jean-Luc Goddard may employ modernist techniques to depict the fragmentation and reification of contemporary society, their works hold no nostalgia for or faith in human progress. Lyotard, one of the principal philosophers of postmodernism, describes the movement as follows:

> [Postmodernism] is undoubtedly a part of the modern... If it is true that modernity takes place in the withdrawal of the real and according to the sublime relation between the presentable and the conceivable, it is possible, within this relation, to distingush the two modes. . . . Here, then, lies the difference: modern aesthetics is an aesthetics of the sublime, though a nostalgic one. It allows the unpresentable to be put forward only as the missing contents; but the form, because of its recognizable consistency, continues to offer the reader or viewer matter for solace and pleasure. . . . The postmodern would be that which, in the modern, puts forward the unpresentable in presentation itself; that which denies the solace of good forms, the consensus of a taste which would make it possible to share collectively the nostalgia for the unattainable; that which searches for new presentations, not in order to enjoy them but in order to impart a stronger sense of the unpresentable. (*The Postmodern Condition*, 79-81)

b) Postmodernism in society and culture

As Lyotard suggests, postmodernism pushes to an extreme the innovations of modernism to reveal the splintered identity of a human subject that was never whole; the underlying lack of knowledge humans have about something we call reality;

the indeterminacy and even futility of our communication. The term postmodernism thus refers not only to art, but also to science, law and morality. The industrial and intellectual boom of the late nineteenth century brought with it both hope and anxiety about technological and social progress. Similarly, the wild dissemination of computerized technology during the late twentieth century brings with it a postmodern despair, and for some, a sense of jubilation that such technology might take over our lives. Postmodern critics such as Lyotard, Jameson and Baudrillard maintain that the proliferation of mass media in contemporary society transforms people into automata who absorb the contradictions of the messages themselves. Commercials and advertisements that tell women to be both feminine and masculine, children to be both dependent and independent, or men to be both violent and caring, for instance, can only lead to a sense of social schizophrenia. In a multimedia age where a complex and contradictory sense of reality is generated by the commodity market and channeled by the media, individuals lose their false and outdated sense of the boundaries between real and unreal; self and other; subject and object.[5]

Much of what postmodern cultural critics maintain is, of course, not entirely new. Karl Marx, for example, one of the foremost theorists of modernity, predicted the increased dependency humans would have upon commodities in order to define themselves. He foresaw the modern dependency upon objects such as expensive cars, cosmetic products, and fancy clothes to define social status and identity. Viewing this dependency as a regrettable inversion between subjects and objects, Marx suggested that humans should consider themselves more important than objects and master those objects through their labor. Marx could not have predicted, however, the extent to which a commodity culture produced by modern technology would define every aspect of human life during the twentieth century. Theorists argue that in contemporary culture, the commodity fetishism depicted by Marx--whereby objects acquire inordinate importance and define our identities as subjects--is pushed to an extreme. Postmodern culture not only inverts the hierarchy between subject and object, but also blurs their distinction.

Commodity fetishism is paralleled by sexual fetishism. In our increasing dependency upon pornographic images, the boundaries between fetish-object and real person have become increasingly thin. Instead of having the rational sense of completeness and mastery of our environment sought by modern philosophers, we experience a loss of personal identity. Our sense of life is reduced to a series of strong and weak "intensities" induced by the mass media and the environment. Life consists of disjointed moments of pleasure and pain detached from a human source and devoid of meaning.[6]

Having lost our sense of identity, we also lose our mastery over human history. The linear and progressive history outlined by modern philosophers such as Hegel, Marx, and Mill is transformed by postmodernists into an aesthetic juxtaposition or *pastiche*: a collage of old and new images and events that disturbs the linearity of time and space assumed by narratives of human progress. As history converts into art, former aesthetic boundaries dissolve. In a postmodern era where the novels of Stephen King are taught in college courses and sold in bookstores next to the novels of James Joyce, high art loses its privileged status and collapses into a market-driven popular culture. The crisis of culture is essentially a crisis of communication. There are no avenues of communication that yield mutual understanding and agreement among human beings; no common criteria that determine value. Humans cannot hope to reach consensus regarding either moral or aesthetic standards because language itself, postmodern critics maintain, is essentially indeterminate.

c) Postmodernism in Language (and its relation to poststructuralism)

In postulating the indeterminacy of language, contemporary postmodern and poststructuralist theories intersect. Both assume that language is essentially self-referential. That is to say, rather than denoting a commonly perceived reality, language only refers to itself. Both theories borrow such assumptions from nineteenth-century structuralist linguistics, particularly the theories of language elaborated by Ferdinand de Saussure.

Let us begin by reviewing some of the key tenets of structuralist scholarship which are relevant to this discussion. First, Saussure defines "language" as a system of signs that are defined *diacritically*, or in a negative relation to one another. For example, the word "man" acquires meaning when contrasted to other words that either resemble it phonetically and graphically (such as "tan" or "van") or conceptually (such as "human" or "woman"). In turn, the two ways in which we have described the resemblances among words--as either graphic/phonetic or conceptual--corresponds to Saussure's distinction between the *signifier* (or the sound/image) and the *signified* (or the conventionally assigned meaning or concept) that comprises a sign or, in this case, a word. The relation between the signifier and the signified is obviously arbitrary. That is, this relation is not motivated by some intrinsic feature of the signifier, signified, or their connection. Instead, it differs from language to language and is "arbitrarily" established by convention.

Saussure's formulation of the sign both envelops and brackets the referent, or the "real" object or concept to which the sign refers. It envelops it because it renders impossible any unmediated or naturalized understanding of the relation between a word and the object it names. Although language does not correspond to things-in-themselves, poststructuralists argue, our perception and comprehension of the material world is made possible only by linguistic systems.

These systems of signification are not only imperfect--since they do not provide us with access to things-in-themselves--but, as Derrida illustrates, are also unstable. In an effort to grasp the "essence" of given referents--for example, "man"--we move from one inadequate approximation to another--for example, to the imperfect synonyms "male" or "human being." This potentially endless chain of signification is restricted only by contextually-specific linguistic conventions. Because the material world is, as far as human beings are concerned, enveloped in our systems of signification, it too becomes understood and deployed as a mode of signification. In this sense, language does not refer only to words, but also to the systems of signification by which we designate concepts, images, and objects.

By using an inclusive concept of language, poststructuralists such as Foucault and Derrida are able to counter the frequent charges that they are setting up a "prisonhouse of language" that ignores the material world and reduces everything to destabilizing plays of signification. For example, in his response to John Searle's critique, Derrida clarifies that,

> What I call "text" implies all the structures called "real," "economic," "historical," socio-institutional, in short all possible referents. Another way of recalling that "there is nothing outside the text." That does not mean that all referents are denied . . . [b]ut it does mean that . . . one cannot refer to this "real" except in an interpretive experience.[7]

Because there is nothing, insofar as human communication is concerned, that is not mediated by linguistic cognitive capacities, poststructuralist critics argue, language is self-referential. That is, as observed earlier, particular words are explained in terms of other words from which they are distinguished or to which they are compared. An inevitable question presents itself: if we cannot grasp the referent--or the objects and events to which our language refers--then how are we able to verify and prove our most fundamental claims about reality? The slipperiness and self-referentiality of language identified by poststructuralist criticism, Lyotard argues, has both epistemological and moral implications. For if we cannot prove and verify with any sense of truth-certainty the nature of our reality, then, he maintains, we may not be able to prove the most obvious and necessary historical and moral truths, such as the fact that the Holocaust took place, that it claimed millions of innocent human lives, and that it was ethically wrong.

d) Postmodernism as presented by this textbook

Having briefly outlined selected features of postmodernism, let me now introduce the arguments and perspectives presented by this book. *Perusals into (post)modern thought* provides a two-fold--both literary and scholarly--introduction to postmodernism. The first half of the book, "Perusals into (post)modern thought," performs "close readings" of important Enlightenment and postmodern texts. The first of these chapters, entitled "Between relativism and universalism: D'Alembert's *Discours Préliminaire*," identifies the continuities between Enlightenment and postmodernist discourses. By analyzing the introduction to the *Encyclopédie*--a text that has come to symbolize the Enlightenment faith in rational thought and in the truth-certainty of empirical knowledge--this chapter argues against a reductive understanding of Enlightenment philosophy as universalist and totalizing. This essay functions as a point of entrance into the Enlightenment versus postmodernism scholarly debates while at the same time contributing to such discussions by attempting to defend Enlightenment thought against (some) postmodern criticism. More specifically, I argue that D'Alembert's text outlines a theory of knowledge that employs a double dialectical process to overcome both the universalism attributed to Enlightenment rationalism and the radical doubt associated with relativism. The second critical essay, entitled "The postmodern need for a philosophy of common sense," furthers understanding of postmodern ethics by exploring the transformations and nuances of Lyotard's own writing: particularly his transition from (what I consider to be) the relativism of his early work, *The Postmodern Condition: A Report on Knowledge*, that operates according to a single dialectical logic, to his attempt to find a mediating path between relativism and universalism in *The Différend: Phrases in Dispute*. The combination of these two chapters, the first focusing on Enlightenment theories of knowledge challenged by postmodernism and the second focusing on postmodern ethics, aims to introduce readers to these two intellectual currents.

The second part of this book, entitled *Hidden glances, silent whispers* makes an abrupt transition in its strategy of reading and presenting postmodernism.   In teaching college courses on the subject, I observed that what draws students to postmodernism is not so much scholarly expositions or debates as the art itself: the novels of Robbe-Grillet, the architecture of Getty, the movies of Goddard. Starting from such particular and vastly different examples, students begin to be curious about their possible correspondence: about the characteristics that lead critics to categorize them as instances of "postmodern" art. Many students also wish to enter into artistic dialogues with postmodern works; to respond to them through their own fiction, painting, music or experimental films. In this book, I have observed the heuristic method preferred by my students. The novella *Hidden glances* supplements the traditional scholarly discussion of postmodernism with my own literary response to selected postmodern texts. While the scholarly essays offer readers a general and, I believe, necessary theoretical background to postmodernism, the fictional section illustrates and problematizes some of the themes and tropes of postmodern literature.

The novella *Hidden glances, silent whispers* was prompted by my reaction to an unfortunately common phenomenon: the gruesome murder of a young woman. As is often the case, the victim was young and beautiful. The press repeatedly displayed her photos and impressed upon viewers and readers that she was well-liked by her friends, respected by her employers, and cherished by her family. This young woman's death incited constant media coverage, hundreds of phone calls of concern, and intensive police investigation. It also provoked sympathy, curiosity and, above all, a sense of morbid fascination with the manner in which sex and violence, and particularly sexual violence against women, are spectacularly interwoven in contemporary American culture.

Life and fiction often resonate, folding upon each other in our imaginations. This murder called to mind not only the themes exploited by popular culture at the time--in movies such as *Silence of the Lambs* and *Natural Born Killers*--but also the plot lines of "high art" movies such as Alfred Hichcock's *Psycho* and postmodern novels such as Alain Robbe-Grillet's *Project for a Revolution in New York*. Most notably, Robbe-Grillet's texts depict various acts of sexual violence against women that are often sensationalized in popular culture--such as sadism, rape, torture, ritual sacrifice and murder--by means of a discontinuous series of narratives that imperceptibly "glide" from one plot line to another and

one narrator to another (who often retains the same name
while assuming a different identity). In so doing, these works
systematically transgress the conventions established by
nineteenth-century realist fiction and perpetuated by contemporary pulp fiction: including unified plot; linear temporal
and narrative sequence, with events happenning in a more or
less chronological order and deviations from this chronology
explained; coherent characterization; supposedly faithful
depictions of real-life events. Robbe-Grillet's texts feature
some of the most important postmodernist techniques,
including a fragmentary, disjointed and multiple plot-struc-
ture, a non-unified and seemingly incoherent characterization,
a mixture of heterogeneous narrators and styles, as well as the
recurrent motif of the fragmentation of women's bodies, used
to typify or accentuate such narrative strategies. It is the very
brutality and banality of his representation of gender, Robbe-
Grillet implies, that enhances the ethical and aesthetic subver-
siveness of his texts. His depiction of sexual violence aims to
block the usual sympathy and reflexive normative evaluation
generally evoked by violent events.

According to sympathetic critics, Robbe-Grillet's works
both reproduce and parody contemporary society's paradoxical fascination with and indictment of meaningless violence,
thus confronting readers with the inherent contradictions and
hypocrisy of their culture. In so doing, Robbe-Grillet's fiction
enables readers to reflect critically upon the inherent conflict
between contemporary values and desires.[8] Yet critical
reflection, particularly that which touches upon the subject of
ethics, can and has, in fact, been turned against postmodern
fiction itself. The connections between gender stereotypes and
(post)modern subversions have been critically examined by
feminist criticism, ranging from Kate Millet's *Sexual Politics*
to Susan Rubin Suleiman's *Subversive Intent: Gender, Politics,
and the Avant-Garde.* Rather than (re)elaborating any
particular argument concerning the affinities between
(post)modern fiction and the representation of sexual violence, my novella takes these by now well-established
arguments as a point of departure for exploring in a literary
fashion what happens once these themes and techniques are
re-appropriated by a female subject to potentially subversive
ends.

The section *Hidden glances, silent whispers* raises ethical questions about postmodern aesthetics by imagining that the serial murderer is a woman who pursues men. This inversion of a familiar plot line is not altogether unique. Films such as *The Deadly Summer*, *Fatal Attraction* and *Basic Instinct* have popularized the figure of the female sexual predator. Noneheless, in these movies the gender dynamics remain stereotyped. The women are beautiful; they seduce the men they pursue by playing upon familiar gender codes, the role of the *femme fatale*. This is not the case in *Hidden glances*. The protagonist of this narrative is a woman whose partner was raped and killed by a serial killer. She does not pursue men primarily out of sexual desire, or even out of desire for power, solace or public attention. She is impelled by largely incomprehensible motivations, as are the male killers in Robbe-Grillet's postmodern fiction. This fictional section intertwines realist and postmodernist literary strategies to trace the heroine's disjointed thoughts and emotions as her actions begin to resemble the behavior of the men whom she most fears and hates.

A simple and senseless gender inversion? Perhaps. But this is precisely what is in question: Can there be a simple reversal of sexual positions when society itself remains so gender-marked? What changes and what remains the same in our evaluation of literature when the gender of the criminal and the victim is reversed in scenerios that depict violence? Hopefully, *Hidden glances* will also encourage readers to consider issues that transcend its particular feminist perspective. The novel provokes many questions, including: to what degree, if any, is ethical criticism of literary works valid? More generally, how do ethics, epistemology and aesthetics intertwine in postmodern theory and art? What are the relations, for example, between the limited knowledge embodied by postmodern narrators and characters (as opposed to the omniscient perspective implied by realist fiction) and the ethical partiality of such characters; their trangression of traditional ethics? Does partial knowledge imply a moral fallibility that leads to evil? These lines of inquiry, which touch upon the interrelations and distinctions between artistic and ethical values, take us back to the source of most of these questions, Lyotard's postmodern theories themselves. Theory and fiction both complement and challenge each other. By creating a *pastiche* of such seemingly incompatible genres, this book seems to observe postmodern subversions of the traditional distinctions between argument and art; objective exposition and distorted representation. I do not, however, intend to subvert these rhetorical boundaries. Rather, by interweaving scholarship and fiction, this work attempts to introduce readers to some of the complex ethical, social and aesthetic issues raised by contemporary postmodern philosophy and art.

---

[1] Jean-François Lyotard, *The Postmodern Condition: A Report on Knowledge*, trans. Geoff Bennington and Brian Massumi, (Minneapolis: Univ. of Minnesota Press), 1984.

[2] Lyotard employs the notion of the Kantian aesthetic sublime to describe postmodern ethics in *The Differend: Phrases in Dispute*, trans. Georges Van Den Abbeele, (Minneapolis: Univ. of Minnesota Press), 1988.

[3] For introductions to and critiques of postmodernism, see *Postmodernism/Jameson/Critique*, Ed. Douglas Kellner, (Washington: Maisonneuve Press), 1989; *Feminism/Postmodernism*, Ed. Linda J. Nicholson (New York: Routledge), 1990; *An Introductory Guide to Post-Structuralism and Postmodernism*, Madan Sarup, (Athens: The Univ. of Georgia Press), 1993; and The Truth about Postmodernism, Christopher Norris, (Oxford: Blackwell Press), 1993.

[4] Susan Rubin Suleiman, *Subversive Intent: Gender, Politics, and the Avant-Garde*, (Cambridge: Harvard Univ. Press), 1990.

[5] See Frederic Jameson, *Postmodernism: Or, the Cutural Logic of Late Capitalism*, (Durham: Duke University Press),1992.

[6] see Gilles Deleuze and Félix Guattari, *A Thousand Plateaus*, trans. Brian Massumi, (Minneapolis: Univ. of Minnesota Press), 1987.

[7] Jacques Derrida, *Limited Inc.*, (Evanston: Northwestern Univ. Press), 1977, 145.

[8] Susan Rubin Suleiman makes such an argument--while also taking into account feminist considerations--in *Subversive Intent: Gender, Politics, and the Avant-Garde* (Cambridge: Harvard Univ. Press), 1990.

Chapter I

Beyond the particular and the universal: D'Alembert's "Discours préliminaire"

In academic circles, the debate between universalists and relativists seems to be as lively today as it was during the Enlightenment, when Denis Diderot and Jean Le Rond d'Alembert disagreed about the nature of truth. Although we may be relying upon Enlightenment philosophy to conduct our own debates about knowledge, the terms of discussion have become more polarized today than they were during the Enlightenment. This essay argues that an important element, namely the middle ground between universalism and relativism, has been left out of contemporary reformulations of Enlightenment thought. Both relativist and universalist theories adopt what I call a "single dialectical" epistemology.[1] According to this paradigm, true knowledge represents the elimination (or negation) of every source of error, social bias, or personal perspective. By way of contrast, I will demonstrate that Enlightenment thought, and particularly d'Alembert's "Discours préliminaire,"[2] elaborates a more nuanced, "double dialectical" theory of knowledge. As I will explain, a double dialectical process combines the quest for truth with an awareness of human differences and limitations. Let me indicate briefly how contemporary criticism has reduced Enlightenment epistemology to a single dialectical relation between truth and error and, consequently, why we need to reconsider Enlightenment epistemology.

On the one hand, objectivist theories claim that the producers of knowledge have the cognitive ability to describe the universe as it really is, not only as they perceive it to be from either a personal or an anthropocentric perspective. Objectivist epistemologies thus imply that the producers of knowledge are (or could become) unbiased in their quest for truth. Such theories also assume that rational individuals share a transhistorical, permanent set of standards that enables them to convey knowledge. Objectivist epistemologies are consequently also universalist because they posit one true way of perceiving the world.

Jürgen Habermas' theorization of communicative action represents one of the most noteworthy scholarly efforts to defend the universalist legacy of the Enlightenment. To establish the validity of empirical and rational knowldedge, Habermas observes a single dialectical process. In *The Theory of Communicative Action*,[3] he maintains that "A judgment can be objective if it is undertaken on the basis of a *transsubjective* validity claim that has the same meaning for observers and nonparticipants as it has for the acting subject himself"(9). I call Habermas's definition of truth "single dialectical" because the critic represents knowledge as the result of a process of selective negation and incorporation. To reach a transsubjective consensus about the content of truth and the process of acquiring knowledge, a person or community must eliminate all sources of error--such as personal bias, emotional investment, and selfish interests--while at the same time incorporating those methods or facts which have stood the test of time.

Universalist scholarship such as that of Habermas not only seeks to preserve the universalist legacy of the Enlightenment. It also reacts against the perceived threat posed by cotemporary scholarly movements that attempt to refute universalism and retrieve the particulatist tendencies of Enlightenment thought.[4] Influential critics such as Michel Foucault and Jean-François Lyotard attribute the notions of truth and falsehood to relations of power rather than to objective standards of validity. Relativist theories assert that there are practically an infinite number of acceptable ways of acquiring knowledge. Although some forms of knowledge may gain more cultural value than others, no knowledge is demonstrably superior to others.

Foucault has been one of the most thorough critics of universalist Enlightenment epistemology and its contemporary legacy. Nonetheless, I would argue that his theory of knowledge also relies upon a single dialectical model. Like Habermas, Foucault defines truth as the negation of human bias and error. In the famous chapter "Man and his doubles" in *The Order of Things*,[5] Foucault comments upon the apparent paradox of the human condition. On the one hand, he states, humans aspire to objective knowledge. On the other hand, he adds, we remain trapped in a human body and mind that reduce our quest for absolute truth to a limited and fragile knowledge:

> Man, in the analytic of finitude, is a strange empirico-transcendental doublet, since he is a being such that knowledge will be attained in him of what renders all knowledge possible. ... For the threshold of our modernity is situated not by the attempt to apply objective methods to the study of man, but rather by the constitution of an empirico-transcendental doublet which was called man. (*The Order of Things,* 318-319)

If knowledge is defined in terms of a single dialectical process that eliminates all limitations, biases and errors, then Foucault is correct to state that man is trapped in a double bind. According to the logic of the single dialectic, to attain truth, we are compelled to project a super-human subject: either by means of the transsubjective communication that eventually leads to universally valid claims (as suggested by Habermas) or by means of the metaphysical projections (be they religious, social or scientific) critiqued by Foucault. While Habermas finds the multiplication of perspectives a path to objective truth (to a more comprehensive unity, consensus),

Foucault ultimately rejects the impossible division of the human subject and lapses into relativism. If humans cannot transcend their anthropocentric limitations, he reasons, then no true knowledge is possible.

What is wrong with the present opposition between objectivism and relativism? Along with critics such as Richard Bernstein, who aim to find a path in between relativism and objectivism, I believe that if we accept either universalist or particularist epistemology, we have little hope of answering the most perplexing questions about human existence.[6] In their crudest form, universalist theories of knowledge permit no genuine debates about truth-claims. The assertion that a given statement is--or should be regarded as--universally true reduces all disagreements to errors or misjudgments. Conversely--but equally dangerous for the pursuit of knowledge--relativist theories render not only the search for truth but also the transmission of information itself meaningless. If all truth claims were indeed nothing but a series of competing language games, then the notion of validity would be either reduced to relations of domination-- where one regime of truth unjustifiably reigns over others--or transformed into inconsequential and sophistical verbal exchanges. Relativism thus eliminates all efforts to present rational, or even acceptable, justifications for statements, beliefs and actions. A good theory of knowledge, I believe, must avoid both of these extremes while also incorporating the useful elements of both. On the one hand, like universalist theories, it should enable critics to distinguish valid from invalid statements and to offer good justifications for such distinctions. On the other hand, like relativist theories, it should incorporate a multiplicity of perspectives and acknowledge human limitations.

In "The Discours préliminaire," d'Alembert proposes such a theory of knowledge by outlining a dialectical process that combines aspects of universalism and particularism while ultimately overcoming both. By way of contrast to objectivists, d'Alembert does not believe that humans can attain unmediated knowledge. At the same time, unlike relativists, he does not give up the quest for (local) truths:

> Far from wishing to obscure a truth which is recognized and undisputed even by Skeptics, I

will leave it up to enlightened Metaphysicians to develop its principle. It is up to them to determine, if possible, the degree of knowledge observed by the soul in its first step, as it is simultaneously pushed, so to speak, and restrained by a host of perceptions which, on the one hand, propel it toward external objects, and on the other hand, belong only to the soul, seeming to circumscribe it within a narrow space from which it cannot escape" (D.P., ii, my translation)

How can humans know that the reality they perceive is objectively true? To answer this question, d'Alembert first dismisses as disingenuous the type of skepticism that casts doubt upon all human knowledge. After negating skepticism, d'Alembert proceeds to negate objectivism. According to d'Alembert, the question of whether our anthropocentric knowledge is objectively true is an unanswerable question. As Foucault would later argue, humans cannot step outside of themselves to verify the accuracy of human perception. Human knowledge, d'Alembert suggests, occupies a space between complete certainty and doubt. To overcome the impasse between relativism and objectivism, d'Alembert doubles the single dialectical process that structures this opposition. He envisions a new relationship between truth and error which, borrowing Luce Irigaray's terminology, I will call a "chiasmus" or a "double dialectics."[7] Let me now explain how a double dialectical process operates and how it improves upon a single dialectical epistemology.

As we have seen, in a single dialectical relationship the concepts of universalism and relativism are created by means of a process of mutual negation. Once trapped in this single dialectical opposition, philosophers are faced with the unpalatable option of choosing either relativism or universalism. By way of contrast, reading these concepts in terms of a double dialectics would suggest that the categories of particularity and difference are not only semantically interrelated, but also inseparable. By depending upon the negation of particularities, the category of the universal simultaneously incorporates the concept of the particular. The same logic applies to the semiotic formation of the particular by means of the negation of the universal. The twin goals of achieving a pure universal by eliminating all particulars or, conversely, of celebrating only differences by negating the universal are unachievable according to the logic of any dialectical process, be it Hegelian or chiasmic.

There is one major difference, however, between the single and the double dialectics. The single dialectic creates a binary hierarchy where *only* one term acquires value by negating the value of the other. Universalists create "objective knowledge" by eliminating all subjective circumstances and opinions. Likewise, relativists produce subjective knowledge by dismissing the possibility of founded agreement. By way of contrast, the double dialectics enables both interrelated terms-- the particular and the universal--to attain what I would call "positive identity." By a "positive identity" I mean that both terms are defined through the simultaneous incorporation and negation of the other term. When the universal and the particular are produced by means of a single dialectical process that privileges only one term and excludes the other, there is no real possibility for open-ended but non-relativistic theories of knowledge. Only when both particularist and universalist claims are granted an equivalent value can we hope to arrive at a philosophical scheme that overcomes the hierarchical dichotomy of universalism and particularism without renouncing either category. Without an appreciation of the notion of difference as essential to the notion of sameness--meaning not only as essential to its definition but also to its critique--we cannot avoid epistemological and ethical absolutism. Likewise, without an appreciation of the notion of universality functioning as a check on the economy of difference, we cannot avoid epistemological and ethical relativism.

As we shall see, the "Discours préliminaire" provides readers with the tools to question both universalist and particularist claims about knowledge by engaging them in a productive mutual critique. For d'Alembert, the universalist belief that human beings can produce true knowledge that is subject to verification and agreement does not necessarily contradict the assumption that such knowledge is mediated and relative. The "Discours" grants that knowledge depends upon and may change according to human cognitive tools, biases, and cultural contexts. At the same time, the text also suggests that knowledge, when acquired through the right methods, yields an accurate *anthropocentric* perception of the world. By navigating a course between relativism and universalism, the *Discours préliminaire* encourages the human quest for accurate descriptions of the world while at the same time allowing for open-ended debates about their accuracy and value.

1. The *Encyclopédie* in the context of contemporary scholarly debates

Why do I regard d'Alembert's "Discours préliminaire" as an optimal point of departure for changing the way we interpret Enlightenment epistemology? First, because I consider this text to be representative of the richness of Enlightenment debates about the nature of truth. The "Discours" introduces the objectives of one of the most important Enlightenment projects, the *Encyclopédie*. No doubt, as numerous critics point out, the highly diversified articles of the *Encyclopédie* cannot be reduced to d'Alembert's view of the project.[8] Nonetheless, the "Discours" functions as a prospectus that indicates what many of the Enlighteners proposed to do in their joint enterprise. Second, as Daniel Brewer has shown, d'Alembert's introduction elaborates the distinctly modern[9] and nuanced understanding of knowledge and value that emerged during the French Enlightenment. This legacy cannot be described solely in terms of universalist thought. Undoubtedly, the tendency toward universalization plays an important role in Enlightenment philosophy. Along with a process of exclusion of the particular to create the false unity of universal concepts, however, we also encounter in the *Encyclopédie* self-critical elements that undermine universalist paradigms.

Scholars generally agree that the French Enlightenment cannot be reduced to a universalist logic. Most critics, however, tend to juxtapose the epistemological openness of some Enlightenment philosophes with the dogmatism of others. According to contemporary criticism, Diderot's work serves as a model of an open-ended epistemology.[10] Conversely, d'Alembert's writing is described as trapped in a closed universalist framework that is not far removed from Cartesian rationalism.[11] In response to such scholarship, I will identify the openness and internal contradictions of d'Alembert's epistemology. Before I explain how my argument differs from and expands upon previous scholarship on the subject, let me describe briefly some of the arguments that resemble my own.

Several influential scholars have emphasized the self-consciously contradictory elements of Enlightenment epistemology. In *Diderot: Le Labyrinthe de la Relation*, for example, Pierre Saint-Amand analyzes the tension between the *Encyclopédie*'s attempt to establish indubitable foundations for human knowledge and its skepticism toward all foundational thought. He argues that the metaphors of the labyrinth (*le labyrinthe*) and the world map (*la mappemonde*) captures this tension. The labyrinth functions as an analogue for the disorder and ultimate incomprehensibility of nature. Conversely, the world map symbolizes the human effort to master both the unruliness of nature and the multiplicity and contradictions of human perception. The labyrinth therefore sketches a relativist epistemology riddled by the confusion of the universe and the incommensurable variety of human representations. Conversely, the world map outlines a universalist epistemology that purports to offer accurate descriptions of the world. The term "complexity," Saint-Amand demonstrates, captures the *Encyclopédie*'s attempt to reconcile order and disorder, certainty and doubt:

> Complexity means simultaneously order and disorder, process. The term also retains its semantic closeness to complication, which is to say that in a system there is quantifiable information, large groups, randomness, a code which escapes us. Finally, complexity represents not so much a term as a structure: order-disorder-paradox. (my translation)[12]

Saint-Amand's reading of the *Encyclopédie* in terms of its philosophical complexity suggests that the tension between order and disorder we encounter in its articles exceeds the logic of mere contradiction. On one level, this tension organizes the entire (static) structure of the text, which juxtaposes the partial and often contradictory information provided by the individual articles with the overarching attempt to provide the truth of nature and society as a whole. On another level, the tension between order and disorder, fragment and whole, motivates a (dynamic) intellectual process that incites generations of readers to question the various truth-claims proposed by the *Encyclopédie*.

Christie V. McDonald's *Dialogue of Writing: Essays in Eighteenth-Century French Literature*[13] and James Creech's *Diderot: Thresholds of Representation*[14] further explore the implications of the *Encyclopédie's* tendency to present knowlege both as representation--and therefore subject to human bias and distortion--and as unmediated truth itself. According to Creech, "The 'Discours préliminaire' expresses the well-known Enlightenment program that for d'Alembert no less than for us was the 'true nature' of the Encyclopedic project. But it also writes large the impossibility of these founding ideological a prioris that contribute its 'true nature' (its identity as Encyclopedia), thus undermining itself to a remarkable degree" (10). If the *Encyclopédie* undermines its own truth-claims by arguing that all knowledge, even the most scientific, is ultimately a form of representation, does it therefore lapse into epistemological relativism? In other words, we are led to ask, to what extent does the *Encyclopédie* undo its main goal of providing a better kind of knowledge than pre-Enlightenment texts?

This is precisely the question posed by Daniel Brewer's *The Discourse of Enlightenment*. Brewer asks:

> If the eighteenth-century Enlighteners sought their freedom by refusing the paradigms and principles that unshakably grounded knowledge in religious and metaphysical terms, do they undo in the process the foundation of knowledge in general, including that of their own epistemological systems? If they reject the universals that underpinned the ethics, esthetics, and social theory of a prior age, what of the ultimate ground of their own theoretical enterprises in such domains?[15]

Brewer answers his own question by arguing that, for the Enlighteners, questioning the objective foundations of knowledge did not conflict with their project of providing more valuable forms of knowledge. In other words, Brewer argues, the Enlighteners wished to have it both ways. They combined a skeptical attitude toward the process of acquiring knowledge with an objectivist quest for truth:

> If the problem of defining the Enlightenment critically marks the limits of modern philosophy, it is because philosophy can be modern only by becoming caught in what could be called the double bind of Enlightenment. . . . The knots of this double bind begin to tighten as the eighteenth-century Enlighteners endeavor to free themselves from the fetters of what they call ignorance, superstition, and religious dogma. They attempt to produce knowledge at its most useful, insisting above all on the arbitrary status of any way of representing knowledge.[16]

I would like to explore further the implications of this seemingly contradictory Enlightenment epistemology, which other scholars have described in terms of its complexity, the symbolic tension between metaphor and metonymy, and the double bind between unmediated truth and distorted representation. As noted, I argue that the seemingly paradoxical epistemology of the "Discours préliminaire" can be explained in terms of a dialectical process that combines aspects of universalism and particularism while ultimately rejecting both. In so doing, the "Discours préliminaire" goes beyond the poor alternative of either forsaking the possibility of true knowledge or accepting closed definitions of truth.

2. Displacing Philosophical Precursors: Empiricist versus/and Rationalist Epistemology

For both critics and enthusiasts of Enlightenment thought, the *Encyclopédie* offers a logical starting point for an investigation of how representations of the subject intersect with distinctly modern means of producing knowledge. No other body of texts provides greater insight into the systems of classification of knowledge produced during the Enlightenment in France than the *Encyclopédie*. Initially, the *Encyclopédie, ou dictionnaire raisonné des sciences, des arts et des métiers* (1745-1772) was conceived by its editors, Denis Diderot and Jean Le Rond d'Alembert, as an imitation of Ephraim Chambers's two-volume *Cyclopaedia* (1728). Although its editors envisioned a small work, the *Encyclopédie* turned out to be a vast and revolutionary project.[17] Rather than faithfully recording acquired knowledge, it generated an epistemological system that provided a new understanding of human moral and political identity. The *Encyclopédie* did not, however, completely reject previous intellectual history. As Michel Foucault illustrates in *The Order of Things*, the *Encyclopédie* built upon and helped undermine Cartesian rationalism.[18] D'Alembert introduces the *Encyclopédie* by tracing the intellectual history of this project. Appropriately, he spends a great deal of time acknowledging Descartes' influence as well as the *Encyclopédie*'s departure from rationalism. Descartes, he explains,

> ...was undoubtedly wrong in accepting the notion of innate ideas. Had he retained from the paripatetic sect the only truth it taught concerning the origination of ideas from the senses, perhaps the errors, which blended with and undermined this truth, would have been harder to extract. At least Descartes dared to teach the learned to escape the yoke of scholasticism, opinion, and authority: in other words, the prejudices of barbarism... If he ended up believing that he explained everything, at least he began by doubting everything. The arms we employ to attack him belong to him even if we turn them against him. (xxv-xxvi, all citations of this text are my translations of the original *Discours Préliminaire*)

Certainly, d'Alembert observes, the Cartesian method, given its reliance upon the notions of innate ideas and theologically guaranteed truths, may not have provided the right foundations for his own rationalist-materialist theory of knowledge. Nonetheless, he qualifies, the Enlighteners could build upon elements of the Cartesian tradition. By engaging in a methodical doubt that questioned former (Scholasticist) methods of acquiring knowledge and, furthermore, by insisting upon modes of demonstration based upon phenomenological experiences, the Cartesian method provided the eigtheenth-century sensationalists, materialists and empiricists with the means of simultaneously validating and questioning their own methods and assumptions.[19]

Although I will not offer a detailed analysis of Descartes' *Discours de la Méthode* (1637), I would like to encapsulate briefly some of the features that proved indispensable to d'Alembert's self-critical, and often anti-universalist, epistemology. As we recall, Descartes attempted to find truth-certainty about our perception of ourselves and of the world. He hoped to eliminate all sources of error by placing under methodical doubt both the accuracy of perception and the assumptions of Scholastic philosophy. We could say that Descartes' methodical doubt observed a double dialectical process, moving first from false universals to relativism, then from relativism back to a truer form of universal knowledge.

True knowledge, observes Descartes, can only be attained by rejecting (or negating) the false universals associated with both commonplace knowledge and Scholastic epistemology. This process of elimination of misleading certainties leads Descartes to doubt everything except, of course, his own ability to doubt.[20] After having discarded dated and false universals, Descartes is left without a strong foundation for knowledge. He lapses momentarily into the epistemological relativism of the subjective self (or *cogito*), whose only claim to knowledge remains the ability to think. Describing human beings in terms of this minimal function does not, however, satisfy Descartes' quest for truth-certainty.

To attain objective knowledge of the universe, the philosopher proceeds to endow the subjective self with some generalizable qualities and criteria of validation. He groups these qualities and criteria together under the notion of "clear

and distinct ideas." Consequently, after having rejected
universalism by interjecting a relativist perspective, Descartes
dispels radical doubt by moving from the particular back to
the universal. Universal standards, or what he calls "moral
maxims," are formed by means of the negation of the
relativism associated with the plurality of views and the
unreliability of human perception that he had postulated
earlier. It would seem as if Descartes were contradicting
himself. He is not, however, because the universalism he rejects
is not the same as the one he proposes. As we remember,
Descartes used relativism to reject false universals. He then
proceeds to imagine a better form of universalism to displace
his momentary (and disingenuous) relativism. As an architect
of rationalist epistemology, Descartes rebuilds the foundation
of truth by positing the validity of "the laws and the customs
of his country," and, above all, by "firmly holding on" to faith
in God. For Descartes, the divine functions as the ultimate
universal guarantee of the validity of human knowledge.

God becomes the standard of universal truth by being
defined as the contrary of the relativistic *cogito*. According to
Descartes' dialectical model, the divine lacks (or negates) all
the imperfection, particularities, and contingencies that
characterize the human.[21] The philosopher thus employs the
figure of God to re-validate, one by one, the certainties he has
placed under methodical doubt, including the existence of the
self, the external world, and true knowledge. If we adopt a
dialectical logic, it follows that if man is imperfect, then God is
perfect; if man is finite, then God is infinite; and if man has
partial knowledge, then God, his creator, must have complete
knowledge. Insofar as human beings are created by a perfect
and all-powerful divinity, Descartes deduces, it cannot be that
all of our faculties are deceptive. Such reasoning leads the
philosopher to his (in)famous conception of humans as beings
whose souls share God's perfection but whose bodies or senses
are imperfect and unreliable. This dualist ontology reflects
the two sides of the double dialectical process Descartes
followed to dismantle prejudice and rebuild truth. The first
dialectical movement, established through a process of
methodical doubt that negates older models of validity, leads
Descartes to describe human sensory perception as relative
and hence unreliable. Conversely, the second dialectical
movement, established through a process of universalization

that negates former sources of doubt, leads Descartes to depict the soul as the faculty that generates "clear and distinct" and hence accurate perceptions of the world.

In the next step of his proof, Descartes mobilizes the idea of God to describe human beings as composed of both fallible body (the source of unreliable, relative knowledge) and infallible soul (the font of universal truth).[22] The philosopher then proceeds to outline a rational process that compensates for the fallibility of sense perception.   Nonetheless, as Descartes' many critics indicate, the two sides of human nature are never fully reconciled.   Descartes provides no satisfactory explanation of how soul and body communicate so well that, rather than the soul interpreting the unreliable sensations perceived by the body, misleading sensory perceptions are corrected by the soul. The double dialectical movements between universalist and particularist claims pursued by Cartesian philosophy consequently do not produce a stable synthesis between doubt and knowledge. Instead, they yield a sublation, or partial incorporation and negation, of both relativism and universalism.   Cartesian philosophy thus embodies the beginnings of a double dialectical process. On the one hand, such a theory uses particularist claims to question universalist certainties.   On the other hand, it also uses universalism as a regulatory ideal that dispels relativist doubts. This is precisely the double movement developed further by d'Alembert.

3. D'Alembert's Epistemology: Beyond the Particular and the Universal

D'Alembert avows that he is particularly drawn to the self-critical aspects of Cartesian philosophy. He notes approvingly, "If he [Descartes] ended up believing that he explained everything, at least he began by doubting everything. The arms we employ to attack him belong to him even if we turn them against him" (xxvi). D'Alembert's statement suggests that Descartes can be regarded as the founder of a form of critical reasoning that inaugurates the beginnings of modernity.   So far I have noted that, in claiming that empiricism relies upon preceding rationalist methods of producing knowledge, d'Alembert acknowledges the "genealogical" filiation between rationalism and materialism.

Let me now elaborate what d'Alembert means by such a genealogy and how it relates to the problem of universalist versus particularist epistemologies. To explain the interpenetration of rationalist and materialist methods, d'Alembert proposes a definition of genealogy that identifies both epistemological ruptures and affinities among different fields of study:

> The first step we have to take in this research is to examine the genealogy, so to speak, and the filiation of our knowledge, the causes which produced it and its distinguishing characteristics: in other words, to arrive at the origin and generation of our ideas.(i)

Like Descartes, d'Alembert maps out the domain of knowledge by negotiating between particularist and universalist assumptions. Genealogical classification, proceeds d'Alembert, if it is to be both comprehensive and sufficiently detailed, must follow a hermeneutic process that constantly mediates between the universal and the particular:

> The work whose first volume we are presenting today has two objectives: as an *Encyclopédie*,it should illuminate, as much as possible, the order and connections of human knowledge; as a *Dictionnaire raisonné des Sciences, des Arts et des Métiers*, it should identify the general principles which establish each Science and each Art as well as identify the most essential details of each branch of knowledge. (i)

On the one hand, as an encyclopedia, the *Encyclopédie* must ascertain the order and connections among different domains of human knowledge. The text attains such a level of comprehensiveness and generality only when it excludes, by observing a dialectical process, the particular features of each field.

On the other hand, d'Alembert continues, as a dictionary, the *Encyclopédie* must also focus upon the individual features of each field. The text delves into details only when it excludes, following an opposing dialectical movement, the intersections and connections among different disciplines. Establishing a double dialectical relation between the particular and the general, the *Encyclopédie* thus presents a system of knowledge that provides more information than does the sum of its parts. Because the text juxtaposes and compares the arts and sciences, d'Alembert can assert that the different disciplines "aid each other, and consequently a common thread ties them together" (i). He qualifies, however, that maintaining an equilibrium between the particular and the general remains a difficult task: "If it is often difficult to reduce each Science or Art to a small set of rules or general principles, it is equally difficult to contain within one system the infinitely diverse branches of the human sciences" (i). Given that d'Alembert acknowledges the difficulty of systematizing information, we are led to ask: What unifies the "infinitely varied" articles of the *Encyclopédie* into a coherent and systematic tree of knowledge? Or, to paraphrase Christie McDonald, what is the epistemological relation between the fragment (the particular) and the whole (the universal) established by the "Discours"?

D'Alembert answers this question by explaining, "The encyclopedic order does not suppose that all the Sciences relate directly to one another. They are branches of the same trunk of human knowledge. Often these branches do not have an immediate connection, and many of them are connected only by the trunk itself" (xix). What unifies knowledge therefore is not so much the inherent links among different fields as human cognition itself. Knowledge, d'Alembert observes, is necessarily anthropocentric. Human beings produce and classify their descriptions of the world, thus transforming the contingency and disorder of nature into a seemingly organic tree of knowledge. By describing knowledge in terms of the arbitrary systems of classification that organize the *Encyclopédie*, however, d'Alembert could, indeed, be interpreted as arguing that human knowledge is relative.[23] As carefully as he avoided universalist epistemology, however, the philosopher sidesteps relativism by adding,

> [The encyclopedic order] consists of gathering information in the smallest possible space and

of placing, so to speak, the Philosopher above
this vast labyrinth in an elevated spot from
which he can perceive simultaneously the main
Arts and Sciences, ascertain in a glance the
objects of his speculations and the operations
he needs to perform upon these objects;
distinguish the branches of human knowledge,
the points which unite or separate them; and
even distinguish the secret paths which bring
them together.(xv)

Having exposed the arbitrary nature of knowledge by showing
its dependency upon competing systems of classification,
d'Alembert proceeds to reclaim its universalist foundations.

Although knowledge may not be objective, he maintains,
neither is it relative. Human beings should be able to
distinguish between valid and invalid methods of producing
information. The best system of classification, d'Alembert
suggests, is one that eliminates the disorder of the world and
of human perception. Once we pursue a dialectical process
that eliminates all particularities and contingencies from the
production of knowledge, we are left with a singular and
seemingly universal perspective. D'Alembert compares this
perspective to a philosophical bird's eye view of the world.
The universal knower imagined by d'Alembert, however, does
not provide an objective description of the world. Such a
subject presents instead the most comprehensive and elegant
representation of the world: meaning, as Brewer has illustrated, one which is best grasped by and most useful to human
beings.[24] To explain the seemingly contradictory proposition
that knowledge can be both true and non-objective,
d'Alembert draws one of the most well-known analogies of the
"Discours." Knowledge, he states,

It is a kind of World Map that should show the
main countries, their position and their
interdependency, the straight path that
connects them—a path which is often cut by a
thousand obstacles; that is known in each
country only by its inhabitants and travelers,
and that is only illustrated by very detailed
maps. These specific maps would be the very

different articles of the *Encyclopédie*, and the
tree or represented system would be the World
Map. (xv)

By employing the metaphor of a totalizing *mappemonde* to
correlate the articles of the *Encyclopédie*, d'Alembert appears
to observe a dialectical process that displaces one form of
epistemological universalism (objectivism) with another
(anthropocentric universalism). As we recall, objectivism
asserts that human descriptions of the world capture the way
the world is. More modestly, anthropocentric universalism
claims that, although humans may not be able to perceive the
universe accurately, there is only one valid human perspective
of it. D'Alembert quite literally embodies this perspective in
the figure of "the philosopher [placed] above this vast
labyrinth in an elevated spot from which he can perceive
simultaneously the main Arts and Sciences" (xv).

This philosophical bird's eye view, d'Alembert explains, is
universal because it is shared (potentially) by all human
beings. The philosopher epitomizes the privileged universal
subject not because he has superior innate faculties, but
because, unlike most human beings, he devotes his intellectual
abilities to the pursuit of knowledge. At the same time,
d'Alembert's epistemology implies that, insofar as other
human beings do not share the opinions of the (imaginary)
universal subject, their knowledge can only be partial,
incomplete, and erroneous. Difference thus becomes
reincorporated into sameness. If all humans, indeed, if
whatever is essentialized as human nature itself, share cognitive
abilities that enable them to have the same knowledge of the
world, then this knowledge cannot be considered relative. On
the contrary, at least from a human perspective,
anthropocentric knowledge can be accepted as not only
reliable, but also as universally valid. Let us now examine how
d'Alembert first establishes, and then proceeds to undermine,
the universality of human cognition. To do so, we must return
to an earlier part of the "Discours," where the philosopher
elaborates a definition of being that complements his theory
of knowledge.

After describing the *Encyclopédie*'s genealogical method,
d'Alembert portrays the human subject capable of producing
such knowledge. He observes,

> Our knowledge can be categorized as either
> direct or dependent upon thought. Direct
> knowledge is that which we obtain
> immediately, without any act of volition....
> Knowledge that depends upon thought is
> acquired by uniting and combining direct
> knowledge.(i-ii)

Like Descartes, d'Alembert describes the materialist subject in terms of his physical and mental operations. Rather than conceptualizing the "homo duplex" ontologically as a split between perfect soul and imperfect body, however, d'Alembert divides man epistemologically in terms of two complementary means of acquiring knowledge. By means of direct and immediate sensations, we, human beings, perceive ourselves and the external world. In turn, our rational or "reflective" faculties select, combine and interpret sensory data. To guarantee the validity of those interpretations, however, d'Alembert must first establish that the sensations which are organized by our rational faculties are reliable themselves.

The materialist philosopher plans to avoid the episte-mological trouble encountered by Cartesian rationalism by assuming, rather than attempting to prove, the reliability of sense perceptions: "Nothing is more incontestable," d'Alembert maintains, "than the existence of our sensations; thus to prove that they are the principle of all our knowledge, it suffices to prove that they could be: because, according to Philosophy, deductions that are based upon facts or recognized truths are preferable to those that are based upon hypotheses, even ingenious ones" (ii). This statement, however, remains ambiguous. It is not altogether clear: What is incontestable according to d'Alembert--the fact that we have sensations or the fact that our sensations accurately depict the world we perceive? D'Alembert's assertion that, in order to show that sensations serve as the reliable foundation for knowledge, it suffices to prove that they *could* serve as such, does not solve his problem. Logically, showing that a phenomenon is possible does not prove that it occurs. Readers are thus confronted with two options. They can either regard d'Alembert's proof as unsatisfactory, or they can accept his founding of knowledge upon sense perceptions as axiomatic. By openly acknowledging his philosophical weakness--namely, that the validity of his assertions cannot be demonstrated--d'Alembert creates a paradoxical epistemology that contains the germ of its own critique. Starting with this rather unfoundational foundation, the philosopher continues to detail what humans can learn from their sensory experience.

Like Descartes, d'Alembert maintains that our first awareness is of our existence. "Our sensations, even if they are not distinguishable, first make us aware of our existence; from this we got our first reflections, that is to say, from the thinking principle that constitutes our nature and is not different from us" (ii). He elaborates, "The second form of knowledge which we owe to our sensations is the existence of external objects, among which belongs our body, because it is, so to speak, exterior even before we have distinguished the nature of the reflective principle in us" (ii). Another question presents itself in light of d'Alembert's account of the interaction between body and mind. If, like Descartes, he describes the body as external to the "reflective principle in us" then how do mind and body interact to provide reliable sensory impressions? Is there any relation, or, more strictly, a correspondence, between the way we perceive the material world and the way the world is?

Once again, d'Alembert interjects doubt rather than certainty into his apparently universalist theory of knowledge. He insists that there is no demonstrable correlation between our sensations and the objects we perceive: "In effect, since there is no relation among sensations and the object which causes them, or at least to which we attribute them, it seems that we cannot find the linking principle that connects them. Only a kind of instinct, more certain than reason itself, can make us overcome such a great gap" (ii). As before, he asks readers to assume the correspondence between perception and objects of perception as axiomatic. Adopting a conversational tone, he assures readers that even the most skeptical philosophers no longer question this correlation. His goal is neither to question "a truth which is recognized and undisputed even by Skeptics," nor to proclaim the objectivity of human knowledge, a problem that he leaves it up to the "enlightened Metaphysicians to develop its principle" (ii). Time and again, the "Discours préliminaire" undermines the possibility of certain knowledge of the world. It does so by negating the correspondence between world and perception (which, d'Alembert maintains, cannot be empirically shown or logically proven) while simultaneously asserting the credibility of such a belief (humans should act as if it were true).

Having undermined objectivism, d'Alembert proceeds to undermine the anthropocentric form of universalist epistemology as well:

> Just as in the general maps of the world that we inhabit, objects are more or less close to one another, and present a different sight depending upon the point of view of the Geographer who constructed the Map, so the form of the encyclopedic tree depends upon the perspective from which we consider the literary universe. We can thus imagine as many different systems of human knowledge as there are World Maps; and each of these systems might have advantages that the others lack.(xv)

By excluding all universal standards from the production of knowledge, d'Alembert moves even closer to epistemological relativism. Human knowledge, he claims, is not unitary after all. What seems to be a good description of the world from one perspective is a poor description from another. Ultimately, humans cannot agree upon the philosophical bird's eye view postulated earlier. Systems of classification themselves are dependent upon the points of view of those who have produced them. Consequently, d'Alembert argues, adopting classically relativist terminology, we can imagine as many systems of classification as there are ways of seeing the world from various locations. Each perspective has certain advantages that the others lack. Does it follow that all "world maps," or all methods of acquiring knowledge, are equally (in)valid?

No, it does not, d'Alembert asserts, once again introducing universalist standards into his momentarily relativist theory of knowledge. To offset relativism, he proposes some criteria of distinguishing good from bad systems of classifications of information. At the same time, he stands by his former claim

that even the best forms of knowledge cannot provide
unmediated access to the truth:

> Whatever the case may be, the tree of
> knowledge that offers the most links and
> connections among the Sciences is preferable,
> without a doubt, to all others. Yet can we flatter
> ourselves of capturing it?... The universe is
> nothing but a vast Ocean, whose surface is
> covered with a few islands of different sizes,
> whose connections to the continent remain
> unkown.(xv)

The epistemology d'Alembert presents through a series of
dialectical moves from (objectivist and anthropocentric)
universalism to relativism plausibly intertwines faith and doubt
in the validity of knowledge. The philosopher reiterates that
the encyclopedia which can offer the most elegant
connections among the various disciplines it presents is,
indeed, preferable to the others. Nonetheless, the information
conveyed by that encyclopedia can be improved upon by
future generations. By acknowledging that, like all human
creations, the *Encyclopédie* is subject to error, d'Alembert
expresses the Enlighteners' sense of intellectual modesty and
openness to competing visions of the world. At the same time,
the "Discours" suggests that without criteria of validity--that is,
without some more or less shared yet negotiable standards--
debates about the nature of truth or reality become
meaningless. In combining a genuine quest for universal
truth with the relativist acknowledgement that such a truth may
never be reached or, at least, that there may be several paths
which can lead to it, the *Encyclopédie* offers a useful
alternative to the dilemma of choosing between relativism and
universalism. This open attitude toward knowledge has
implications for both ontology and ethics. If truth claims
must be argued for and can be contested, then definitions of
humanity as well as the boundaries between ethical and
unethical behavior are also subject to discussion.

In my analysis of the "Discours préliminaire," I began to
sketch such an alternative cultural logic that selectively
combines, rather than displaces, universalist and particularist
standards. By arguing for the necessity of developing a

double dialectical relation between particularist and universalist epistemological claims, I have attempted to offer a
possible answer to Naomi Schor's timely question: "what
becomes of universality in an era of ever more marginal
subjectivities, ever more anti-universalist gender disorders?
According to what logic can particularism flourish, severed
from the universal? Or to put it more bluntly: is the universal
worth saving?   Or, more cautiously: is there anything in the
classic conception of the universal that is worth saving?"[25]
My essay maintained that both particular and universal
standards are worth saving and, moreover, that the two should
be regarded as not only conceptually but also normatively
inseparable. Along with critics such as Richard Bernstein[26]
and Naomi Schor,[27] I argue that the goal is not to eliminate
the universal, but "to arrive at a new universal that would
include all those who wish to be included and that would
above all afford them the opportunity to speak universal while
not relinquishing their difference(s)."[28]   Although I do not
claim (or even wish) to prescribe the content of this new
universality, I have suggested that one way in which it can be
produced is by establishing a double dialectical relation
between particularist and universalist standards.   In a double
dialectical process, the category of difference serves to ward
off epistemological and ethical absolutism. Analogously, the
category of universality serves as a flexible standard used to
negotiate the limits of human knowledge.   The critical and,
indeed, necessary tension between universalist and relativist
standards that we encounter in Enlightenment texts has
produced a complex philosophical system that could be
regarded as a fruitful beginning for the elaboration of an
epistemology, ontology and ethics of our postmodern world.

---

[1] I am using the term "dialectic" in a Hegelian sense, to indicate a
conceptual and historical process of achieving progress by means of a
series of sublations (or the selective negation of undesirable qualities
and incorporation of desirable qualities into a later stage of
development). I describe d'Alembert's thought as "dialectical" because I
believe that Hegel systematized most elegantly a process that was
already employed by previous philosophers, including d'Alembert.

[2] All references to the "Discours préliminaire" are to the facsimile of the first edition published between 1751 and 1780 of the *Encyclopédie ou Dictionnaire Raisonné des Sciences des Arts et des Métiers*, (Stuttgart-Bad Cannstatt: Friedrich Frommann Verlag, reprinted 1966). The translations into English are my own. This essay has appeared previously in *Eighteenth-Century Studies* (April, 1999).

[3] Jürgen Habermas, *The Theory of Communicative Action*, vol. I, trans. Thomas McCarthy (Boston: Beacon Press, 1989).

[4] Because relativism maintains that there are multiple particular versions of the truth, I will use the terms relativism and particularism interchangeably.

[5] Michel Foucault, *The Order of Things*, trans. A. Sheridan (New York: Random House, 1970).

[6] Richard Bernstein, *Beyond Objectivism and Relativism: Science, Hermeneutics and Praxis* (Philadelphia: University of Pennsylvania Press, 1983), 3.

[7] The essay "Beyond the particular and the universal" has previously appeared in *Eighteenth-Century Studies* (April, 1999). In this essay, I am borrowing the term "double dialectics" from Luce Irigaray's *An Ethics of Sexual Difference*, trans. Carolyn Burke and Gillian C. Gill (Ithaca, Cornell Univ. Press, 1984). In this work, Irigaray uses the terms "chiasmus" or the "double dialectics" as a metaphor for a yet unachieved sexual reciprocity and equivalence between women and men. For an exposition of Irigaray's use of the metaphor of a "chiasmus" or "double dialectique" to critique Hegelian thought, see my forthcoming book, *Gender and Citizenship : A Genealogy of Subject-Citizenship in Nineteenth-Century French Literature and Culture* (New York: Rowman and Littlefield, 1999). I employ the term "double dialectics" not as a metaphor, but as an explanation of a semiotic process that overcomes binary hierarchies, including the one established between the relative and the universal.

[8] Wilda Anderson's *Diderot's Dream* (Baltimore, Johns Hopkins Univ. Press, 1990), for example, juxtaposes Diderot's and d'Alembert's visions of the *Encyclopédie*. She states: "Diderot's meditations, in the famous article 'Encyclopédie,' demonstrates this split. This article constitutes a quite striking example of what will come to be the characteristic Diderotian writing stance resulting from his notion of all activity as interaction, for it is a direct response to d'Alembert's 'Discours préliminaire'" (5). By underscoring the non-dogmatic nature of d'Alembert's "Discours," this essay engages in an implicit polemic with

Anderson's book and other works that read the "Discours" as epistemologically closed.

[9] Daniel Brewer, *The Discourse of Enlightenment in Eighteenth-Century France: Diderot and the Art of Philosophizing* (Cambridge: Cambridge University Press, 1993).

[10] For example, in *Diderot: Le Labyrinthe de la Relation* (Paris, Librairie Philosophique J. Vrin, 1984), Pierre Saint-Amand argues: "Dans l'article 'Encyclopédie,' Diderot reprend les images du tableau, de la carte, de la mappemonde, images qui, chez d'Alembert, banalisent la complexité encyclopédique (dispersion des articles) en ligne droite. Mais Diderot n'adopte pas une position aussi théologique que celle de son collaborateur. Au point de vue pyramidal de d'Alembert, position idéale du philosophe faisant tournoyer autour de lui la carte des sciences, Diderot oppose un univers multicentré, essentiellement leibnizien"(71).

[11] Wilda Anderson persuasively demonstrates the continuity between Cartesian rationalism and d'Alembert's materialist rationalism in *Diderot's Dream*.

[12] Saint-Amand, 16.

[13] In *Dialogue of Writing: Essays in Eighteenth-Century French Literature* (Canada: Wilfrid Laurier University Press, 1984) Christie V. McDonald describes the double nature of the *Encyclopédie*--vacillating between fragmentary articles that disperse knowledge to its totalizing project of capturing all knowledge--in terms of the symbolic shifts between metonymy (or the part) and metaphor (or the whole): "Finally, the 'work of the text' is to elaborate a system in which the fragment leads to the whole, in which the dialogue between the articles attests once again to language as communication within a staunchly monologic--or utopian--system. In contrast, the 'text of the work' is that which disrupts the system, isolates the fragment, disperses dialogue into the endless interference of reading with writing, and makes possible only local--not universal--meaning" (88).

[14] James Creech, *Diderot: Thresholds of Representation* (Ohio State University Press, 1986).

[15] Brewer, 5.

[16] Brewer, 2.

[17] As Daniel Brewer documents in *The Discourse of Enlightenment*, by 1772 the *Encyclopédie* comprised seventeen volumes containing 71,818 articles and eleven volumes containing 2,885 plates.

[18] In *The Order of Things*, Michel Foucault argues that Descartes and D'Alembert, or more generally, rationalism and empiricism, share

epistemic foundations. He contends, "One has the impression--and it is often expressed--that the history of nature must have appeared as Cartesian mechanism ebbed... Unfortunately, things do not happen as simply as that. It is quite possible...that one science can arise out of another; but no science can be generated by the absence of another...mechanism from Descartes to d'Alembert and natural history from Tournefort to Daubenton were authorized by the same episteme" (128).

[19] As John C. O'Neal notes in *The Authority of Experience: Sensationist Theory in the French Enlightenment* (University Park: The Pennsylvania State Univ. Press, 1996), the concepts of empiricism, sensationism and materialim overlap, and thus are often used interchangeably. All three theories proposed that knowledge is derived from observation of the phenomenal world. To begin distinguishing these concepts, we might say that empiricim refers to an epistemology which posits that knowledge is derived from experience; materialism refers to an ontology which assumes that the real world is made up of matter (as opposed to ideas,); while sensationism, as O'Neal indicates, refers to a more focused intellectual movement during the Enlightenment that argued for the sensory origin of ideas (smell, touch, sight, hearing). Generally speaking, d'Alembert's epistemology can be called empiricist because it takes into account the knowledge provided by observation. Most often, however, I refer to d'Alembert's epistemology more specifically as "materialist rationalist" because it combines the belief that the universe is physical or material with the assumption that the universe can be known through a combination of abstract reasoning and observation.

[20] Descartes states: "But having learned since my school days that one cannot imagine anything so strange or unbelievable that it has not been said by some philosopher, and, since then, during my travels, having acknowledged that those who have feelings quite contrary to our own are not for that reason barbarians or savages, . . . I could find no one whose opinions, it seemed to me, ought to be preferred over the others, and I found myself constrained to try to lead myself on my own." In the footnotes, I will be citing from *Discourse on Method*, translated by Donald A. Cress (Hackett: New York, 1980), 8-9.

[21] Descartes continues, "For, following from the reasonings I have just given, to know the nature of God, as far as my own nature was able, I had only to consider each thing about which I found an idea in myself, whether or not it was a perfection to have them, and I was certain that

none of those that were marked by any imperfection were in this nature, but that all other perfections were. So I observed that doubt, inconstancy, sadness and the like could not be in him, given the fact that I would have been happy to be exempt from them. Now, over and above that, I had ideas of several sensible and corporeal things; for even supposing that I was dreaming and that everything I saw or imagined was false, I still could not deny that the ideas were not truly in my thought"(19).

[22] Descartes deduces, "since I had already recognized very clearly in my case that intelligent nature is distinct from corporeal nature, taking into consideration that all composition attests to dependence and that dependence is manifestly a defect, I therefore judged that being composed of these two natures cannot be a perfection in God and that, as a consequence, God is not composed" (19).

[23] The arbitrary aspects of the *Encyclopédie* I am refering to include its alphabetical order, the differing human opinions and perspectives expressed by the text, and its selection of certain qualities and functions of objects as opposed to others.

[24] As Brewer observes in *The Discourse of Enlightenment*, "The order of things in the *Encyclopédie* is determined above all by the status accorded them as belongings, by their usefulness to an ordering subject. Things in the encyclopedic text do not simply exist, they are meant to be used, and the products of their use are their value, which is one reason for the countless images of tools and machines in the encyclopedic plates" (19).

[25] Naomi Shor, *Bad Objects: Essays Popular and Unpopular* (Durham: Duke University Press), 1995, 16.

[26] See, for example, Bernstein's attempt to move philosophical debates beyond the impasse of relativist and universalist ethics in *The New Constellation: The Ethical-Political Horizons of Modernity/Postmodernity* (Boston: MIT University Press),1993.

[27] I am referring in particular to Naomi Schor's call for a reevaluation of the value of some open universalist norms in her essay "French Feminism is a Universalism," found in *Bad Objects*.

[28] Schor, 26.

Chapter II

The postmodern need for a philosophy of common sense

By questioning the assumptions of traditional epistemology and ethics, postmodern philosophy casts doubt upon the certainties established by Enlightenment and modern thought.[1] We no longer believe, postmodernists tell us, that there is a stable, coherent and rational self who observes the knowable and predictable (Newtonian) laws of nature. Once we reject the assumption that reason connects us to some universal truth, we also reject the belief that reason and science offer a stable foundation for knowledge and ethical behavior. That is to say, if we are not motivated by the necessary and rational laws of nature, then our forms of knowledge are neither transcendental nor objectively true. Science loses authority as the paradigm of all knowledge. The knowledge we create, including scientific knowledge, is contingent, the product of partial and perhaps erroneous points of view. There is no guarantee that the information we acquire corresponds to anything true or real. In turn, if absolute truth does not exist, then obeying the so-called laws of reason does not yield social and personal freedom. Acting rationally, in other words, does not make human beings independent or free. According to some postmodern critics, including Foucault and Lyotard, the discourse of truth represents only a highly effective means of exercising power. There is no neutral form of knowledge: all knowledge is partial and self-serving. Knowledge is therefore socially beneficial only to those who know how to persuade according to the most effective "language games." The truth of claims made in the name of knowledge is validated contextually, according to the rules and premises of a particular language game. Postmodern criticism thus tends to translate the discourse of truth into relations of power and claims about reality (things-in-themselves) into theories of representation (descriptions of reality).

In this book, I alluded to the response of postmodern philosophy, particularly that of Jean-Francois Lyotard, to Enlightenment ethics and epistemology. While in previous chapters I discussed how postmodern philosophy challenges Enlightenment thought, in this conclusion I would like to consider both the possibilities and the limits of postmodernism in addressing some of the fundamental questions of human existence. Taking Jean-Francois Lyotard's main works, *The Postmodern Condition* and *The Differend*, to be significant examples of postmodern philosophy, I will briefly examine these texts with the following questions in mind: How does postmodernism represent the relation between truth and error? What are some of the blindspots of postmodern epistemology? What is the basis and nature of moral conduct according to postmodern philosophy? What are the limitations of postmodern ethics? I believe that Lyotard's works provide a good point of departure for broaching these questions not only because they offer a sophisticated elaboration of post-modern philosophy, but also because, in my estimation, they help readers realize the necessity of some of the Enlightenment tenets they reject. By this I do not mean to imply, as some critics do, that the shortcomings of postmodern theory make Enlightenment philosophy appear more appealing by comparison. Rather, I argue that postmodernism criticizes the limits of Enlightenment thought only to confront its own limitations. I will chart this philosophical route, which brings Enlightenment and postmodern philosophy to a full circle, by following Lyotard's shift from a single to a double dialectical model of epistemology and ethics.

In *The Postmodern Condition*, I argue, Lyotard pursues a single dialectical logic that negates objectivism to arrive at a relativist epistemology. In *The Differend*, the author attempts to follow the same relativist path by rejecting the assumptions that buttress universal morality. By choosing to focus on the events of the Holocaust to substantiate his relativist theory, Lyotard illustrates that even in circumstances where universalism appears to be the only acceptable position--such as the observations that the Holocaust took place and that it was morally wrong--its assumptions and logic are open to questioning. In other words, by negating universalism even in one of its most compelling instantiations, *The Differend* seems to arrive at moral relativism. Nonetheless, in my analysis of the chapter "The Differend," I will show that the text's conclusion is far from conclusive. In the chapter "The referent, the name," Lyotard attempts to negate relativism and rebuild a shared epistemology and ethics upon non-universalist foundations. In so doing, he charts a double dialectical process similar to the one elaborated by the Enlightenment and modern texts I have considered so far. Modern and postmodern discourses, rather than being only opposites, sometimes resonate in the effort to provide plausible answers to the most challenging human questions.

1. A single dialectical epistemology: Lyotard's *The Postmodern Condition*

In *The Postmodern Condition: A Report on Knowledge*, Lyotard announces the beginning of a new era, characterized by the questioning of every discourse that aims to discover and communicate the truth, including theology, science, social science, ethics and law. He defines the modern period as deploying "any science that legitimates itself with reference to a metadiscourse"(xxiii). By way of contrast, he describes the postmodern attitude as "an incredulity toward meta-narratives"(xxiv). Postmodern culture undermines the certainties that enabled modern societies to function by "making an explicit appeal to some kind of grand narrative, such as the dialectics of Spirit, the hermeneutics of meaning, the emancipation of the rational or working subject, or the creation of wealth" (xxiii). According to Lyotard, the fields of science, social science and humanities, which began to be differentiated during the Enlightenment, are similarly governed by rhetorical rules that aim at reaching mutual understanding and consensus. In all cases, "truth-value is deemed acceptable if it is cast in terms of a possible unanimity between rational minds: this is the Enlightenment narrative, in which the hero of knowledge works toward a good ethico-political end--universal peace" (xxiv). Enlightenment metanarratives thus depend upon, and in fact generate, a subject of knowledge that is unified, coherent, rational and supposedly works toward a common goal with all other similarly constructed subjects. [2]

To arrive at such unity, Lyotard suggests, the subject must eliminate (or negate) all logical inconsistencies, partial affiliations, disruptive psychological impulses, and social differences from its being and social context. In other words, the modern subject develops as a result of a single dialectical process that negates the fragmentation, incoherence, difference and partiality that would disturb social unity and consensus. Consensus, Lyotard concludes, "does violence to the heterogeneity of language games. And invention is always born of dissension. Postmodern knowledge is not simply a tool of the authorities; it refines our sensitivity to differences and reinforces our ability to tolerate the incommen-surable"(xxv). Lyotard thus sets up a binary opposition between Enlightenment and postmodern discourses. Postmodern discourse represents everything that the Enlightenment attempted to eliminate from its system of thought: difference, heterogeneity, and dissension. Since postmodern philosophy is generated by the negation of Enlightenment universalism, it stands to reason that postmodernism emerges from a homologous, but inverse, single dialectical process to the one that created Enlightenment concepts. That is to say, the heterogeneity and multiplicity of postmodern discourse is created by the negation of the unity and consensus attributed to modern discourse. My question is: being a product of the same dialectical process, how is postmodern discourse an improvement over Enlightenment thought?

I raise this question because Lyotard clearly believes that postmodernism represents such an improvement. Just as numerous Enlightenment and modern philosophers, ranging from Condorcet to Marx, believed in the inevitable progress of the human being and society, so Lyotard believes in the inevitable dissemination of postmodern forms of knowledge. "The nature of knowledge cannot survive unchanged within this context of general transformation. It can fit into the new channels, and become operational, only if learning is translated into quantities of information" (4). Despite the heterogeneity of postmodern discourses, Lyotard suggests, all regimes of knowledge can be described in terms of a unitary theory of power: "Knowledge in the form of an informational commodity indispensable to productive power is already, and will continue to be, a major--perhaps *the* major--stake in the worldwide competition for power... A new field is opened for industrial and commercial strategies on the one hand, and political and military strategies on the other" (5). While political interests, contexts and linguistic rules may differ, the objective of all discourses remains the same: the manifestation of power. "For it appears in its most complete form, that of reversion, revealing that knowledge and power are simply two sides of the same question: who decides what knowledge is, and who knows what needs to be decided? In the computer age, the question of knowledge is now more than ever a question of government" (8-9).

If all knowledge can be reduced to one overarching goal or effect, we are led to ask, then how does Lyotard's epistemology differ from the unitary epistemology he ascribes to modern thought? Lyotard addresses such a question by suggesting that the universalist discourse of the Enlightenment established itself upon the foundation of truth. By translating truth into power relations, postmodern philosophy dispels such criteria of legitimation.

While not having the same foundations as Enlightenment discourse, postmodernism nonetheless produces similar effects. Both Enlightenment and postmodern discourses gain authority by distinguishing different communities and areas of competence from those who fall outside of their boundaries. By creating and then negating the difference of others, Lyotard maintains, privileged communities establish control over less privileged ones. So far, Lyotard is not saying anything different from Franz Fanon or Edward Said. He observes that some communities use knowledge to deny the humanity of others and thus establish social and moral authority. At the same time, he generalizes Fanon's and Said's observations. According to Lyotard, all discourses are equally complicit--even if differently effective--in the quest for power. From this assumption it follows, for instance, that colonialist and anti-colonialist discourses are equally right or wrong. Discourses that claim to espouse truth and moral correctness, Lyotard further suggests, only aim to produce social hierarchies: "What is a 'good' prescriptive or evaluative utterance, a 'good' performance in denotative or technical matters? They are all judged to be 'good' because they conform to the relevant critieria (of justice, beauty, truth, and efficiency respectively) accepted in the social circle of the 'knower's' interlocutors. ...The consensus that permits such knowledge to be circumscribed and makes it possible to distinguish one who knows from one who doesn't (the foreigner, the child) is what constitutes the culture of a people" (19).

Postmodern philosophy exercises its own demystifying form of power to undo the influence of universalism. To distinguish postmodernism from its philosophical precursors, Lyotard insists that he is only depicting a cultural process that is already underway rather than prescribing what should occur. "In contemporary society and culture--postindustrial society, postmodern culture--the question of the legitimation of knowledge is formulated in different terms. The grand narrative has lost its credibility, regardless of what mode of unification it uses, regardless of whether it is a speculative narrative or a narrative of emancipation" (37). Since the Second World War, Lyotard observes, the dissemination of technology has encouraged Western societies to focus on pragmatic aspects of life. Modern cultures have given up the search for a universal truth that is not related to immediate results. Consequently, in the wake of modernization, a new pragmatics of knowledge has emerged. This way of life is made possible by a multiplicity of language games that are "heteromorphous, subject to heterogeneous sets of pragmatic rules" (65). Because postmodern societies have abandoned the search for universal truth, Lyotard reasons, "...it seems neither possible, nor even prudent, to follow Habermas in orienting our treatment of the problem of legitimation in the direction of a search for universal consensus" (65). My question is: does Lyotard's description of postmodernism arrive at universalism by means of a different route?

Given that he has translated both epistemology and ethics into a unitary theory of power, Lyotard has undermined the supposed heterogeneity of postmodern narratives. While seeming to negate the concepts of sameness, unity and consensus to proclaim the value of difference, postmodern philosophy arrives at something resembling a common cause which levels the differences among postmodern discourses. The problem with Lyotard's version of postmodernism stems from its single dialectical negation of universalism. By setting postmodernism in direct opposition to universalism, Lyotard replaces the modern discourse of value (truth, right) with a postmodern discourse of power which is similarly unitary. In pursuing this single dialectical logic, Lyotard's rendition of postmodern philosophy is no more equipped to distinguish among (the ideological effects of) postmodern discourses than he is attuned to the nuances of Enlightenment thought (which he dismisses as universalist). The need to distinguish among discourses, however, becomes all the more obvious when claims about truth intersect with assumptions about morality. This is precisely the problem with which Lyotard grapples in his later book, *The Differend: Phrases in Dispute.*[3]

2.   The need for double dialectics: Lyotard's *The Differend*

The Differend examines the foundation of ethics by inter-twining in a surprising dialogue radically different kinds of relativist and universalist discourses. The text places side by side citations from Plato's *Gorgias* with articles from Nazi revisionist historians and journal excerpts from Holocaust victims. To increase the confusion, the citations are removed from their textual and historical contexts. What is the reader to make of this *pastiche* of historical information intermingled with philosophical speculations about the nature of morality and knowledge? This is precisely the question raised by Lyotard's *Differend*. To induce readers to think about their ethical and epistemological assumptions, Lyotard begins by defamiliarizing moral discourse. His presentation of ethical problems is not only unconventional, but also downright shocking. While some critics celebrate *The Differend* as a highlight of postmodern philosophy, others express a sense of outrage at its unabashed ethical relativism. Cristopher Norris is one of the most outspoken critics of postmodern philosophy. In his essay "Kant disfigured", Norris cautions:

> [M]oral relativism if taken seriously can offer no defence against obnoxious creeds just so long as there is (or once was) a "language-game," "discourse" or cultural "form of life" wherein they enjoyed some measure of communal assent. ... Only thus can one explain Lyotard's attitude in the face of right-wing "revisionist" arguments like that of Robert Faurisson, namely, that since no witnesses survive who can vouch directly for what happened inside the gas-chambers at Auschwitz, therefore the historical record is mute on this point and we should treat all talk of the Holocaust as--so far as we can possibly know--a conspiracy devised to denigrate the Nazis and promote the Zionist cause. The most obvious response to such sophistries would be to point out their manifestly absurd major premise, their willful disregard for other (massively documented) sources of know-ledge, and the presence of a blatant motivating

interest, or crudely propagandist intent, which
explains both their flouting of their factual-
historical rules of evidence and their utterly
unprincipled ethical stance. (249)

Whether one is impressed with or outraged by Lyotard's
approach to ethics, the question remains: Why does the author
choose to buttress postmodern ethics on one of the most
sensitive examples of the need for universalist thought?   An
obvious answer would be that the true test of moral relativism
is its response to incidents that seem unquestionably evil. This
explanation, however, does not fully explain *The Differend's*
ability to provoke readers. For not only does the text level the
distinction between right and wrong, but it also inverts this
relation by expressing moral disapproval at the suppression of
what are conventionally regarded as immoral points of view.
As Norris continues to explain,

For Lyotard, however, such [moral] arguments
are beside the point, assuming as they do that
Faurisson is playing by the same evidencial or
ethical rules, or that opponents have the right
to arraign this "discourse" from a standpoint of
assuredly superior probity and truth. By so
doing, Lyotard maintains, they commit an
injustice, a suppression of the "differend,"
which deprives their case of any genuine claim
to rectify Faurisson's similar breach of ethico-
discursive responsibility. This seems to me a
very clear (and shocking) example of what can
go wrong when moral relativism is joined to an
extreme version of the incommensurability
thesis derived from post-structuralist and other
theoretical sources. For the result of such
thinking is to level the difference between
truth and falsehood, good and bad faith,
respect for other people's honestly-argued
convictions and an attitude of all-purpose
skeptical doubt which admits any viewpoint--
however ill-founded, prejudicial or malign--as
entitled to its own internal criteria. (249-250)

I cite Norris's position at length precisely because I am highly sympathetic to it. Having a similar reaction to *The Differend*, I searched for a different way to defend the common sense opinion that some acts, including the murder of millions of people, are evil. To do so, I will turn Lyotard's text against itself. My reading of *The Differend* will reveal that, unlike the earlier *Postmodern Condition*, this text does not stop at the rejection of universalist norms to support moral relativism. Rather, in the chapter by the same name, *The Differend* turns full circle and calls for the creation of new moral boundaries. Such moral limits, Lyotard cautions, cannot be established upon universalist foundations, which, as noted, he believes are only a product of nefarious power relations. To arrive at a non-universalist postmodern ethics, Lyotard pursues a double dialectical process that negates both universalism and relativism. My essay will argue, however, that Lyotard never presents this new moral order--nor does the narrative logic of his text help readers envision it--because he does not perform a full sublation of both relativism and universalism. That is to say, *The Differend* incorporates and negates aspects of relativism while only negating aspects of universalism.

To understand the path that Lyotard attempts to chart between relativism and universalism, let us see what the author means by "the differend." The author offers three definitions of the term, all of which pertain to a pragmatic, legal, context. Ethics and law, the author suggests, are inextricably intertwined. Ethics serves as the foundation of law, while law provides the concrete framework for the negotiation and enforcement of ethical values. The differend occurs when ethical values cannot be negotiated because of the absence of agreed-upon laws. In the first instance, "a differend would be a case of conflict between (at least) two parties, that cannot be equitably resolved for lack of rule of judgment applicable to both arguments. One side's legitimacy does not imply the other's lack of legitimacy." (xi) A common example of such a situation would be the political debates of the United Nations. In the absence of any higher judge or agreed-upon law, there is no way to resolve the moral and political conflicts that result from cultural and personal differences without excluding, and thus wronging, some nations.

The second example of an insoluble moral conflict is "the case where the plaintiff is divested of the means to argue and becomes for that reason a victim" (9). To be able to adjudicate a moral conflict, Lyotard suggests, we need not only shared laws, but also the fair presentation of the conflict itself. When one side cannot speak for itself and affect the judgment of the arbiter or judge as much as the other side, the moral conflict becomes undecidable. This description of the differend leads us to the third meaning of the term. Sometimes a legal conflict cannot be decided equitably because the judge or jury is biased. While unbiased judgment is certainly assumed in the legal systems of democratic nations, Lyotard suggests, such fairness is an unattainable regulative ideal. Given that ethical evaluation in a legal context is always biased, Lyotard asks, what becomes of moral judgment?

To answer this question, the author turns to the epistemological basis of moral judgment. Legal systems may be imperfect, but human beings have other ways of distinguishing right from wrong. Much as Hume systematically undermined confidence in causal reasoning, so Lyotard turns to epistemology to unravel common sense assumptions about what constitutes adequate proof. Furthermore, just as Hume demonstrated that causal reasoning may lead us to plausible, but far from certain conclusions, so Lyotard wants to demonstrate that legal evidence only shows that an event probably occurred. There is no way to prove a crime occurred and to identify with certainty the perpetrator. If ethics has no epistemological foundation that supports alleged facts, Lyotard further suggests, then normative judgments are arbitrary.

Lyotard's testing ground for the intersection between epistemology and ethics is the following question: How can we prove that a horrific historical event--such as the Holocaust--took place? Furthermore, Lyotard pursues, given the manner in which we are able to prove that this event happened, how can we judge it as right or wrong? Assuming that epistemology and ethics are two facets of the same universalist discourse, Lyotard attempts to invalidate proofs that the Holocaust took place--by showing the shaky ground on which such proofs rest--to unsettle our confidence in moral judgments.

He begins by juxtaposing two kinds of narratives that declare truth-certainty: the traditional historical account which argues that the Holocaust took place and it was evil and the Nazi revisionist account which states that there is no evidence of the Holocaust. Both traditional and Nazi historians, Lyotard suggests, pursue a single dialectical process to establish the certainty of their conclusions. As we recall, a single dialectical narrative depends upon the creation of binary hierarchies. Following this logic, traditional historians rely upon different kinds of evidence to negate all doubts and support the position that the Holocaust certainly happened. Homologously, Nazi historians reject all evidence to invalidate proofs of the Holocaust.

By way of contrast, Lyotard's *Differend* observes a double dialectical logic that gives both universalism and relativism equal value. Both objectivists and relativists, Lyotard suggests, cannot fully substantiate their arguments. This is perhaps the most disturbing element of Lyotard's text: while many people with different political agendas have denied the existence of the Holocaust, few have suggested that traditional and Nazi historical accounts of this event are equally (in)valid. To chart this double dialectical path between complete certainty and doubt, Lyotard considers the occurrence of the Holocaust from an epistemological and ontological perspective.

3) Epistemology: Negating truth-certainty

Traditional historical accounts of the Holocaust generally rely upon three types of narrative evidence: a) the testimony of Holocaust survivors and victims; b) the testimony of eye witnesses; and c) interpretations of victims's trauma and resulting silence. As noted, Lyotard juxtaposes such accounts with the denials of Nazi revisionist historians to invalidate both arguments.

a) Personal experience

Lyotard begins by analyzing evidence based upon personal experience, including diaries such as the one written by Anne Frank. Personal accounts are assumed to be at least partially generalizable. That is to say, traditional historians argue that the experience of one individual can say something about the experience of others. By way of contrast, Nazi historians reject this assumption. They present the following argument: "You are informed that human beings endowed with language were placed in a situation such that none of them is now able to tell about it. When they do speak about it, their testimony bears only upon a minute part of this situation"(3). While traditional historians maintain that the testimony of Holocaust surviors provides reliable evidence of what millions of other victims experienced, Nazi revisionist historians assert that it is unique to the experience of that single victim. Lyotard selectively rejects and incorporates elements of both arguments. *The Differend* suggests that historians must be particularly careful about making generalizations based upon personal experience without going so far as to conclude that personal narratives can never be generalized. Lyotard's juxtaposition of two positions that claim truth-certainty raises the question: to what degree is personal experience and narration reliable evidence for a mass phenomenon? Leaving this question open for the reader to decide, Lyotard moves on to consider the credibility of the victim.

A second issue that presents itself in the evaluation of personal evidence is the problem of truth-value. Is the personal account a true, undistorted, representation of the facts? While traditional historians argue that personal accounts of Holocaust victims are reliable, Nazi historians argue that any exaggeration or distortion made in that document renders a personal account untrue. Once again, Anne's Frank diary provides a good example for this debate. Traditional historians have found that Anne distorted many minor facts. Anne herself admitted that she exaggerated the negative depiction of her mother and of the members of the family who shared her hiding place. Traditional historians nonetheless argue that such exaggerations have no bearing on Anne's experience as a Nazi victim. The fact that she might have exaggerated descriptions of her mother has nothing to do with the fact that she had to hide to survive; that she experienced food shortages; that she eventually died in a concentration camp. All these events, historians argue, remain undeniably true. Nazi historians use the same evidence to reach the opposite conclusion. In their estimation, any distortion of facts damages irreparably the credibility of the witness. Consequently, they suggest, nothing Anne wrote in her diary can be trusted. "How can you know that the situation itself existed? That it is not the fruit of your informant's imagination?" they disingenuously ask. (3) Lyotard's narrative once again distances itself from, or negates, both objectivist and relativist positions. Personal evidence, *The Differend* suggests, is neither completely reliable nor unreliable. It is simply inconclusive. Having sublated these two opposed positions, the text moves on to consider a second type of evidence.

b) Witnesses, empirical evidence and logic

Most victims of the Holocaust did not live to write or tell about it. Much of the evidence of mass murders which occurred was gathered from eye witnesses: from the individuals who saw the horror or were asked to work in the concentration camps. The Nazi historians attempt to invalidate eyewitness accounts by constructing the following syllogism:

> To have "really seen with his own eyes" a gas chamber would be the condition which gives one the authority to say that it exists and to persuade the unbeliever. Yet it is still necessary to prove that the gas chamber was used to kill at the time it was seen. The only acceptable proof that it was used to kill is that one died from it. But if one is dead, one cannot testify that it is on account of the gas chamber... [In] order for a place to be identified as a gas chamber, the only eyewitness I will accept would be a victim of this gas chamber; now, according to my opponent, there is no victim that is not dead; otherwise, this gas chamber would not be what he or she claims it to be. There is, therefore, no gas chamber. (3-4)

Nazi historians take as their major premise the assumption that the only way to prove that the gas chambers killed is to have experienced death under those circumstances. Their minor premise is that all individuals who experienced the gas chambers are dead. A second minor premise is that if a victim is dead, he or she cannot speak about it. This chain of reasoning leads them to the conclusion that the fact that the gas chambers were used to kill people cannot be substantiated. Obviously, there are shaky premises in this chain of reasoning. For instance, the assumption that only those who died in a gas chamber can attest to its existence is clearly false. Nonetheless, sophistical logic can lead to the relativist conclusion that, "since the only witnesses are the victims, and since there are no victims but dead ones, no place can be identified as a gas chamber" (5). *The Differend* does not side with the Nazi revisionist historians to suggest that the Holocaust is conclusively unprovable. Nor does it side with traditional historians who trust eyewitness accounts. Rather, *The Differend* provides a metacritique of the conceptual tools that enable both sides to make their arguments. Logic, Lyotard shows, can be a double-edged knife that can lead to opposing conclusions. Rather than being an instrument of truth, as universalists assume, logic is a rhetorical tool. Suspending readers once again between certainty and doubt, Lyotard moves on to consider the third type of evidence.

c)   The undecidability of silence

Individuals who experienced the Holocaust expressed themselves in different ways. A few wrote about it. Most victims, however, internalized their pain and remained silent. For historians of the Holocaust, what is not said about this event is as important as what is said about it. The fact that many Holocaust survivors find their memories too painful for words, indicates to many the extent of their suffering. According to Nazi historians, however, not speaking about the Holocaust implies that no suffering occurred: "The survivors remain silent, and it can be understood 1) that the situation in question is not the addressee's business; or 2) that it never took place; or 3) that there is nothing to say about it; or 4) that it is not the survivor's business to be talking about it. Or several of these negations together" (14). Rejecting both historical interpretations, Lyotard uses Plato's *Gorgias* to argue that silence represents a double bind: "The silence of the survivors does not necessarily testify in favor of the non-existence of gas chambers, as Faurisson [the Nazi historian] believes or pretends to believe. It can just as well testify against the addressee's authority..., against the authority of the witness..., finally against language's ability to signify gas chambers (as an inexpressible absurdity)" (14). Faced with silence, the public cannot decide between several plausible but mutually exclusive meanings.

4. Ontology: Negating physical evidence

Having considered the difficulty of proving that an event occurred based upon verbal and narrative evidence, Lyotard moves on to evaluate the most compelling and gruesome proof of the Holocaust: the gas chambers themselves, the trains used to transport millions of people to their deaths, the bits of clothing and hair found in concentration camps, the photographs of emaciated victims. In the second chapter of *The Differend*, entitled "The Referent, the Name," Lyotard examines the nature of physical evidence. Although I will not analyze the rest of Lyotard's text here, I would like to signal some of its main arguments to indicate how the author continues his dialectical path between relativism and universalism. Lyotard first maintains that proofs of reality generally depend upon circular arguments. Tautological arguments tend to run as follows: "I say the gas chambers exist because they were there." Such arguments, Lyotard implies, do not demonstrate anything. From tautologies, "Existence is not concluded. The ontological argument is false. Nothing can be said about reality that does not presuppose it" (32). A second manner in which people substantiate claims about reality is by offering numerous details. The ability to produce details generally convinces individuals that an event occurred. Yet, Lyotard succinctly objects, "Naming is not showing" (33). Details may signal an active imagination rather than proving that an event occured. Lyotard's third ontological argument challenges the belief in the continuity of the subject. Alluding to Descartes's method of radical doubt, Lyotard suggests that there may be no continuity between subjects who were alive in the gas chambers and those who died a few moments later. "The possibility of reality, including the reality of the subject, is fixed in networks of names 'before' reality shows itself and signifies itself in experience" (35). Relatedly, Lyotard proceeds to argue, claims about reality are always vague, if not indecipherable, because language itself is undecidable. Applying Saussurean linguistics to ethical problems, Lyotard indicates that in a diacritical system of language, "Reality is not expressed therefore by a phrase like: *x is such*, but by one like : *x is such and not such*. To the assertion of reality, there corresponds a description inconsistent with regard to negation. This inconsistency characterizes the modality of the possible" (45). If we accept Saussure's argument that human beings communicate by moving from one linguistic approximation (or signified) to another, Lyotard suggests, we are led to the conclusion that we do not have access to the referent (or prelinguistic reality in-itself).

What is left of proof of the Holocaust? If one lends credence to Lyotard's reading, there are no traces of concentration camps; there is no verifiable history:

> Is it up to the historian to take into account not only the damages, but also the wrong? Not only the reality, but also the meta-reality that is the destruction of reality? Not only the testimony, but also what is left of the testimony when it is destroyed (by dilemma), namely, the feeling? Not only the litigation, but also the differend? ... Auschwitz is the most real of realities. ... Its name marks the confines wherein historical knowledge sees its competence impugned. It does not follow from that that one falls into non-sense. The alternative is not: either the signification that learning (*science*) establishes, or absurdity, be it of the mystical kind. (57-58)

To talk about the Holocaust, Lyotard suggests, we must invent new rules of validation that take into account the fact that nothing can be either proven or disproven with absolute certainty. This is certainly a common-sensical conclusion-- pursued by American courts in the clause that a person is declared guilty when the jury is certain beyond reasonable doubt that the accused perpetrated the crime. Nonetheless, Lyotard's interpretation of a double dialectical process, as well as the epistemological and ethical claims he makes, lead to shocking conclusions. As the author himself suggests, the process of negating both relativism and universalism risks falling "into non-sense." Indeed, the conclusion that the Holocaust may not have occurred, that there is no way for historians to prove that it did, is altogether non-sensical. For just as we go to bed each evening expecting to wake up in the morning at the light of the sun--even though, as Hume indicated, we cannot be absolutely sure that the sun will rise--so our societies must function as if some of their most deeply-held moral and epistemological convictions were true.

I have argued that *The Differend* attempts to chart a path between relativism and universalism to create a distinctly postmodern epistemology and ethics. To do so, Lyotard pursues an incomplete double dialectical process that selectively negates and incorporates elements of relativism--and, indeed, arrives at similar conclusions to those of Nazi revisionist historians--without also incorporating elements of universalism. In assessing the reliability of evidence, *The Differend* never incorporates some universalist tenets--such as the criteria needed to distinguish between essential and non-essential facts. According to the logic of Lyotard's reading, Anne's Frank distortion of facts about the boy she fell in love with is as important as if she had lied about hiding from the Nazis. The same can be said about Lyotard's juxtaposition of logical arguments made by traditional historians and Nazi revisionist historians. Having only negated universalism without also incorporating some objectivist standards--such as the distinction between true and false (or plausible and implausible) premises--Lyotard dismantles logic to arrive at a syllogism which resembles that of the Nazi historians. Lyotard and many of his followers would respond that the distinctions between significant and insignificant evidence or between true and false assumptions are a product of universalist language games. While this may be true, I would respond that without such assumptions we cannot function as human societies and risk "falling into non-sense."

Rather than observing a dialectical process to return to a new, "postmodern" form of relativism, contemporary critics are beginning to use a double dialectical logic to re-evaluate common sensical positions and overcome the impasse between relativism and universalism. This philosophical common sense carries with it its own risks. As we have seen, by negating universalism, Lyotard's *Differend* reverted to conventional relativism. Similarly, if contemporary critics negate relativism and incorporate universalist positions too readily, their philosophies risk lapsing into dogma. My reading of Enlightenment and contemporary theories in terms of the logic of the dialectic has not provided a formulaic solution to this dilemma. Rather, my essays propose a method for understanding local answers to the difficult quest for a philosophical equilibrium between universalism and relativism.

---

[1] For a succinct introduction of how postmodern philosophy undermines the tenets of modern philosophy, see Linda Nicholson and Nancy Fraser's "Social Criticism without Philosophy" and Jane Flax's "Postmodernism and Gender Relations" in *Feminism/Postmodernism*.

[2] In this citation, Lyotard is alluding (and objecting) to Jürgen Habermas's theory of communicative action.

[3] Jean-François Lyotard, *The Differend: Phrases in Dispute*, trans. Georges Van Den Abbeele, (Minneapolis: Univ. of Minnesota Press), 1988.

Part II: Hidden glances, silent whispers

The flyer preempted my action. I was about to throw it away, when I glanced over the white, computer-printed paper. It commanded me not to discard it and then gave me some information about a meeting I would have liked to attend. After I read it, I threw it away anyway, but not without some sense of having been caught in the act. I looked around. Did anyone see me? Apparently not. There was no one around the mailboxes. At least no one close enough to read the flyer and know what I was doing.

In fact, I was not doing anything at all. I spent my life watching others. Watching out and looking around. I would have liked to be a voyeur at the meeting described by that flyer. I could not attend the meeting openly. No. The most I could do is be there without being seen. To judge others without being judged in turn. And by this, I don't mean to say that I wanted to be ignored. In some ways, I think I wanted to be at the center of attention without any effort or risk. I wanted to find myself at the center of the room, surveying everyone there like a hidden camera, zooming in, framing close-ups, ignoring some people, focusing on others, producing a scenario that escaped my control. Controlling without giving directions, without touch or interaction, only by means of my invisible and mobile perspective, through partly unmotivated selections and elisions.

Controlling a beautiful woman with long hair by watching her sensuous mouth speak only with silence, smile, move rapidly and incomprehensibly once again, then freeze still for no apparent reason... And cut! Move from the curve of her mouth to the sweeping arch of her arm, that fluid and rapid gesture toward the open window that might have escaped unseen. Along with her veiled movements and thoughts, my camera takes flight to the fresh air outside, tracing the foliage of autumnal trees that eclipse the unheard murmurs of the room with their bright yet somber colors. I feel the crisp air just by seeing the trees strip underneath the blue sky; by following the movements of the people I watch at a meeting where I am not even present; by noting the protective gestures with which they wrap their arms around their bodies as they stand before the open window, as vulnerable and alive to the cool breeze as they are to my sight. Then: cut!

Just like that. Being in control without having to survey my conduct, to avoid faux pas, to be discreet, to try to fit in. I did not want to control the people who would attend the meeting today. No. Controlling others requires too much self-control. It depends upon finding that delicate balance between following and leading others: knowing how to seem to lead them mostly by following their lead. For me, real control meant invisibility, invulnerability to judgment, a congruous mixture of total non-existence and all-pervasive life. Control is similar to the experience of writing for and listening to yourself. There is a certain grandeur and power in loneliness and insignificance. A very fragile power. The kind of power that could be dispelled by any contact, by any interaction. The kind of power that is like a secret: if you keep it to yourself, the illusion works, but as soon as you share it, as soon as you let others penetrate your walls, it ruptures or explodes not with a bang, but with a kind of pitiful obscene noise.

I try to guard my hollow secrets like one holds in a breath of fresh air by not talking or breathing; like one sweeps in a handful of sand and tries not to move so that it would not trickle between one's fingers. And when I breathe or open my clenched fists, I do so slowly and deliberately, using gestures and words that do not express anything except what others already expect to see or hear.

* * *

I walked aimlessly, pursuing any direction, certain that just about any path would eventually take me home. The evening had started to cover the city streets in a quiet gray. People were rushing about me, coming toward me and pushing me away with a force that needed no words or contact, rocking me back and forth in a flux of apathetic confusion. Then it started to rain. The first drops of water externalized my mood without giving it any sense or solace. Someone asked for money in front of the grocery store. Someone else whistled at a woman crossing the street. The whistle jostled me, reminding me that I was not alone, that at any moment one of the figures around me could try to pierce my loneliness with its life, cries, or gestures. I looked around at all the faces moving around me, closed or expressive, attentive or self-absorbed, and felt that the drops of rain clinging to my body were my only companions. I held out my hand to them, hoping to feel their cold and soothing touch, then quickly withdrew it, thinking that I should not beg for sensations I could not offer. I felt the need to find myself at home, to slip quickly and quietly through the crowd, to be enveloped in a familiar and reassuring loneliness.

When I entered our apartment, Isabella was already there. She was reading the local paper, looking concerned and pale as her glance zigzagged through the lines.

Did anything new happen?

I was just trying to make conversation before finally reaching seclusion. Simple words, a friendly hello, a question, any greeting at all, may dispel the tension that is always potentially there, making the room seem gloomy and tense. But despite its friendly tone, my question sounded phony and bland, bringing in the soggy fragments of the outside world that had permeated my coat, my hair, my gaze, my voice. The air inside our living room felt stuffy and wet. Isabella looked up, brushed my face with her eyes to assess whether I expected an answer, then responded with her entire body, like she usually does. Her frizzy hair, her frail and nervous frame, her sad gray eyes became a chorus of sound, color, shape, tension and motion. Nothing new had happened. Events occurred and recurred, differentiable only in nuance and circumstance, determined yet unpredictable, justifiable and comprehensible only in retrospect, and even then, only by those who needed to find or offer answers.

A young woman had been raped and murdered.

I did not want to hear any more about it so I asked: When did this happen?

Yesterday.

So now another woman was found raped and murdered. What did such an event convey? I asked myself. For whom was it telling and significant? Why do we need to narrate and hear about these carefully selected, framed, and edited events? I wondered. If such events themselves make little or no sense, then why do we use them to fill our lives with meaning? Why do we swallow all kinds of narratives in industrial doses, manufactured by different plants, both secular and religious, both fictional and factual? Are we still searching for the lost fragments of an explanation of who we are and what we are doing on this planet? Do we wish to avoid the vacuum of having to produce a reason for existence out of nothing; to struggle against no force; to find no sustenance or air; to have no material with which to construct or shatter dreams?

Pretense joys and pretense pain, transmitted by "their" standardized voices of objectivity--journalists, forensic experts, professors, doctors, lawyers, teachers, mechanics, salespeople, religious and political figures, actors--to "us," the audience of uncaring receivers. "They" are "us" and "we" are "them," and in the invisible space between that transmission and reception of simulated words and feelings, there is no distinguishable language or communication, just different patterns and rhythms of eloquent silence and noise.

Appparently, Isabella was still talking.

...Women...prove...strong....disincentive...threat...men... punishment she said.

I could tell that she needed me to become angry; to promise to become involved in her women's group; to care and act and be just like her, while never ceasing to be myself. Sameness in difference: she only wished for what most of us expect from life. But her expectations never brought us closer, never took us anywhere.

So I usually let her expressions hang in the air, hoping they would dissipate, along with her anxiety, in the ensuing silence.

It feels stuffy here, let's open the window.
No, it will rain inside.
And instead of fresh air or rain, a shower of words and unwanted details flooded the room.
...She was only 23.... police.. bar... suspect... violence....compassion.
This last word puzzled me. It had an interesting ring which made me feel incongruously excited, alert and unhappy. Com-passion? All of a sudden I was holding Isabella, cradling her small nipples in my palms and kissing her open-mouthed into silence, hush Isabella, and as these images flashed before my eyes all I could do was slip quietly into my room and firmly close the door behind me.

* * *

A little peace and quiet.
Closed door, closed blinds, closed eyes:
the world is almost covered by nothingness.
I am alone with Eliza.
A flash of an image coming from nowhere
 and all I can see is red.
He....grabbed...she...frightened....
turned... held...gun....
tenderness...hatred.
A quiet corner...
during mid-afternoon.
Her face... couldn't see him...
covered... cold blood.
Blood, innocence, reason, understanding,
forgiviness, punishment and death.
These words resonate,
run together one after the other,
without making a coherent sentence,
without ever catching up.
And still, he was caught.
200 pounds, short,
dark brown hair,
38 years old and allowed to go free.
Violent record: rape, murder and theft.
Punch, hit, kill, slaughter him...back.
Look into his eyes

and see only anonymous hatred,
masterfully painted in red and white.
Slash the white with the red,
letting them blend together
in long rosy streaks of pain
that purify his tainted being,
then wash his wounds with salt water
to give him a reason for living
in his moment of death.
Remember: if he tries to escape,
pull his scattered pieces together,
and use bits of his flesh
as evidence in court.
Just like they did to her...
Then walk away,
meekly and softly,
carrying your small bag of fading memories
and large burden of unforgettable pain.
Have no regrets.
When you get tired of walking,
run.
When you get weary of running,
hide.
Then, when you can no longer live in hiding,
come forth to lie down
and mourn on the grass
nourished by her former being;
return her to nothingness
by melting her cold skin
with a warm touch of your tender hand.

* * *

A knock on the door interrupted my breathing. I exhaled
"Come in" and Isabella stepped inside.
    You want to talk about it? she asked abruptly. You seem
upset.
    A question interwoven with an affirmative statement which
functioned as an imperative. Typical Isabella style. It's a pity
she's always so apprehensive and tense; if she were more
relaxed she would have a fragile and commanding beauty, in

both manner and appearance, the kind that invites respect and protection, desire and distance, all at once.

No, I don't really feel like talking about anything right now.

You never feel like talking about anything with me, she reproached. And when you do, her voice trailed off with sadness, it's always about the same thing.

What do you mean? I pretended not to understand.

It's always about Eliza, she said softly, for fear of hurting me even more.

I knew what she meant and could relate to her loneliness. She felt as lonely with me as I did with her: and our unhappiness was really my fault. But I felt that there was nothing I could do about it. Nothing. So I just answered in the usual way: I'm sorry, but talking about my feelings right now wouldn't help at all.

I was skeptical about discussing personal problems. I felt that, as the saying goes, we are all alone in suffering and death. In my experience, discussing problems only made things worse. Personally, it made me more aware of the limitations of sharing my experience; of the limits of human compassion. Isabella looked at me unnerved.

Then what will? she asked. How long do we have to go on like this, moving like shadows past one another? Tell me, how long?

Tension and emotion. I always felt guilty for making Isabella suffer for my problems. Yet nothing I could say to her could bridge the growing distance between us; nothing could bring us together. Most of our "serious" discussions ended in disappointment or fights. Looking at Isabella's beautiful face, elongated by my coldness and distance, made me feel worse than ever.

Sorry for bothering you, she announced in an angry voice.

You didn't bother me at all Isabella, I tried to reassure her. But how could I convince her that I cared; that my distance was not a sign of dislike but an attempt to sort out my own world before joining hers? Would she have the patience to understand? Should anyone be expected to have so much calmness and faith?

As I caught her eye, an open wound of hurt and delicate feelings, she looked away and turned to leave. Did she know that she could bother me anytime? But not by asking me to talk about my problems. No. She could disturb my inner world by opening the door with her light touch, slipping inside, and looking at me in a way that made me feel potent and desirable, autonomous and possessed. The way I used to feel before. Before my whole life was shattered by fear, hatred and pain.

* * *

During moments of doubt, I wondered about how I became Isabella's lover. Not even why, a much more complicated question, but how. I could not pinpoint the moment when it happened or even imagine the circumstances which led up to it. I needed, nonetheless, to endow our relationship with some sense of history which would make "us" seem more solid, more together, more real. A sense of timelessness, of imaginary solipsism, enveloped our life together. But this did not feel like the timelessness of eternity but more like that of the ephemeral: a fleeting moment that you have forgotten even before you have realized that something, an event, took place almost simultaneously in your life and hers. How did our existences merge?

I wished to recreate our origins, to generate the womb of our past, in order to believe that our lives together held some future meaning. Without such origins, we, together, could not even begin to exist. We each had our separate worlds, our distinct pasts, our personal desires. And yet, it seemed like we were always together. We had been living together for a few years, talking past each other, evading the other's presence while at the same time seeking each other's empty embraces with the lifeless desire of living ghosts. A contradiction or an incomprehensible dream? I could not tell or remember.

All I could recall is being alone, with my palms plastered to the wet ground of Eliza's grave, a ground molded by rain and intermingled with tears. I felt sad that Eliza could not even enjoy a sunny day during that crucial transition, when her new life began and her old life had ended. I wanted to believe that Eliza would continue to exist elsewhere; that I would continue to speak and caress and need and love her even in death. Without this hope, how could I survive, deserted and alone, all of a sudden, for no reason. I kept searching for a justification for my loss, that inexplicable punishment for a crime I had never committed. I searched for meaning in meaninglessness by gazing at the rotund shapes and somber colors of the clouds, those clouds that held no spiritual power or human compassion. In the emptiness of that vacuum, I repeated the same hollow questions. Why did she have to die? Why did she leave me? Why her? How could I live without her? These questions echoed, louder and louder, more and more painfully, in my empty soul. But they simply couldn't be answered. For a brief moment, I remember making the futile effort of trying to take life and death into my own hands. I plastered my palms to the wet ground, grabbed the earth, and tried to disinter Eliza and save both of us from eternal separation.

One moment I was rooted to the ground of my pain, attempting to dissolve the boundaries between life and death, the next I already had assumed a new life, the life of a stranger, not a continuation of my own. Isabella formed the fulcrum of this new existence whose beginnings I could not remember; whose slow, viscous and disorganized flow seemed to have no purpose for either her or myself.

I realized that Isabella could not be blamed for my sense of estrangement. No. It really wasn't Isabella's fault that I desired her in this nonsensical way, as an impossible substitute, as a total stranger. I needed to love someone the way I had loved Eliza, but my love for Eliza had never ceased, and no one else could fulfill it. So I lived unfaithfully. Unfaithful in my love for Eliza, yes, but more faithless in my efforts to love Isabella.

Isabella sensed our isolation. She often asked me if we would ever become closer; if our relationship would ever work. But she did not seem to expect a positive answer. Perhaps she thought that I was hopeless in my grief. Perhaps she hoped that I would emerge from mourning reborn, with a renewed hunger for life and happiness. I tried not to ask what she thought. She tried not to tell me. Instead of talking or living, I prefered to carry a three-way internal monologue, speaking to Isabella about Eliza and to Eliza about Isabella, enclosing all external life into the tomb of my imagination. Examining the world through this opaque prism, I could remain faithful to Eliza, in a minimal sort of way, that involved no effort, pleasure or risk.

* * *

He said hello, looked at me with small condescending eyes, and told me to lie down on the couch.

I said hello, looked at him with barely disguised resentment, and followed his orders.

He sat behind me. I could feel his knee almost touching my head; I could smell his expensive musky colone. A sense of discomfort prompted me to speak. To say something, anything at all, just to get it over with as quickly as possible. Our meetings always felt like an injection. Nonetheless, I had hope. Maybe this time I would be innoculated. Not from depression or madness, but from its cure. Maybe this time he would tell me to never come back. Maybe he would finally admit that there was nothing else he could do. I wanted to hear that. I wanted to hear that I was so hopeless that even people who were paid to help me could not do it. I wanted to have tried and failed to help myself. I wanted to be left alone.

I asked him what he wished to know about my life. I couldn't see his sardonic smile, but I could sense it in his voice.

He told me that it was up to me. That he was there to listen.

I asked him if everything I said would be interesting to him. Even if I rambled. Even if all that came out of my mouth was senseless jabber.

He told me that I should know better by now. It was the rambling that was most meaningful to him. The problem with me was that I never could ramble. I only constructed algorithmic tales and repeated them *ad infinitum*.

So I began to talk. I talked to fill out the empty time and space around us. I talked to feel like I was making some attempt to understand my life. I talked, above all, because I didn't know what else to do.

I told him that I kept remembering the day I met Eliza. I didn't know how, I didn't know why, but that moment kept interfering with my life, preventing me from swallowing my food, disrupting my sleep, troubling my dreams, interrupting my motions, words and silence.

He asked me why that memory disturbed me.

I told him it just did.

Then I told him that I met Eliza in a flower shop.
He said that he had already heard that story.
I said that didn't matter. I would repeat it again and again.

I told him that I met Eliza in a flower shop. She was dressed in a bright red dress, as red as the rose petals she was gently caressing with the tips of her fingers. She had blue eyes, as blue as the forget-me-nots that peeked at us from their tender green leaves. To me, she seemed to blend into the array of colors, scents, velvety softness and fragility of her environment. All the rest of us, the human beings, did not belong in this fauna of sensation.

He told me that I was romanticizing again, the same way I did when I told him this story the last few times.

I asked him, what else could I do? This is how I remembered the event. This is how I perceived Eliza. I viewed her as a delicate flower that I could gaze at, fascinated, from a distance. The most I could do was touch the flowers she touched, which evoked the velvety feel of her youthful body. I viewed her as a lingering perfume that evoked luxury and passion. The most I could do was bask in her fragrance, which intermingled with the intoxicating scent of flowers.

After awhile, I gathered the courage to ask her a question. I asked her for what occasion she was buying flowers. She smiled, with an embarrased sort of smile, a little timid and crooked, and answered that they were for her boyfriend. I felt a little discouraged but refused to give up. Ah, I said. Shouldn't he be the one buying you flowers? I asked. She became even more embarrased and said that it was his birthday, not hers.

Although she had not asked, I said that I was also buying flowers for my boyfriend. I told her that, by a great coincidence, it was my boyfriend's birthday as well. She laughed and I laughed in response. Then she asked me the age of my boyfriend. I answered that he was twenty years old. How old was her friend? Eighteen.

I did not know it then, but we had given our ages. We were both young, but she seemed much younger than me, not so much in years as in body and experience. Compared to her green youthful body, I felt like a tree trunk with many rings, rings around the eyes, the mouth, the hands, the legs. I felt infinitely old compared to her.

She stopped smiling and looked at me with curiosity. She examined me in a scrutinizing sort of way, which seemed surprising. That look did not correspond to my mental image of her as a naive young girl. She looked me up and down, then probed my face with her forget-me-not eyes. But only for a moment. The next moment she smiled, all radiant and friendly once again, and asked me what the name of my boyfriend was. I did not know how to respond.

For some reason unknown to me at the time, I felt compelled to tell the truth. I did not even think about it much; I just answered that the name of my boyfriend was Jenny. Then I felt that I had made a mistake. That she would find some excuse and promptly say goodbye. Like the others.

She did not. She did not laugh, or change expression, or turn around to leave. She continued to look at me in the same intent and honest way. Then she said that the name of her boyfriend was Allison.

We both laughed. After that laughter followed a hiatus of awkward silence. What else could we do? It seemed like we had already said everything there was to say. And yet I did not want our conversation to end. So I told her that I wanted to know her name. What was her name? I asked.

Eliza. Her name was Eliza.

Then I was quiet. I listened for a long time to his evaluative silence. It had a ring of disapproval. When he finally spoke, he scolded me. Not as a person, but as a subject. Not as a friend, but as a professional. He said that I had not done my homework. I had not allowed my dreams and fantasies to flow out of me. Instead, I condensed them into an infinitely repeatable moment. He said that for an intelligent woman, I was the most boring patient he had ever had. I answered that for an intelligent man, he was the most insensitive psychiatrist I had ever met. Then we set up another appointment.

* * *

As I walked back to our apartment, I began to remember. I remembered why I loved Eliza. I remembered this love in a different way than I had immediately after she died. After her death, I could not even picture clearly Eliza's features. Pain obscured my visual memory. I had to constantly examine

Eliza's pictures, glance at her static and smiling blue eyes, caress the rough texture of her blond hair, in order to recall the person whom I had loved and lost. It seemed like Eliza was no longer a person, but an emotive explosion within me: a sharp inconsolable pain, yes, but also a bouquet of illuminating flashes of shared feelings, memories and dreams.

After a long time, more than a year perhaps, I began to relive episodes of my life with Eliza more vividly. I felt as if our lives had been videotaped and I were watching certain episodes on an invisible screen. Most often, those episodes were part of silent movies, capturing diverse and incongruous scenes: Eliza running in the park and stepping by mistake on the eggs and tomatoes we had brought for the picnic; me chasing her and shaking with anger and laughter at the same time. Eliza bringing me red roses on Valentine's day in front of my colleagues; me thanking her with cowardly embarassment for her nice birthday gift. Eliza telling me about her obsession with the existence of evil and the senselessness of human suffering on Earth; me telling her not to worry about it since it was not yet happening to her.

For some reason, I tended to recall those moments of our lives that juxtaposed our characters in an ironic yet also comical fashion, as if the lightest moments of our pasts were being resurrected as the heaviest and most retrospectively telling moments of my present without her. I suppose this is how the meaning of a life develops: by means of infinitesimally brief reconstructions of a past which emerges out of what seem to be the dark, insignificant aspects of a picture: a negative space that suddenly develops under the exposure of light and time into a vivid image.

I did not know if these photographic memories and filmic moments filled me with more pleasure or pain. It's true that thinking of Eliza made me smile more often than cry, which was all I could do before, soon after she died. But my smile often became a sad ironic grin, almost a scowl, when I thought that she was gone and there was nothing I could do to revive her. This sense of impotence shadowed by guilt gradually assumed the form of a question: Was there anything I could do to correct, even in a minimal sort of way, what had been done to Eliza? This open question, wavering on the brink of a new resolution, constituted the puzzle that would, some day, piece together my shattered life.

* * *

Between the two of us, I was the academic but Eliza was the true intellectual. She loved art, poetry, philosophy. She loved them open-mindedly and open-heartedly, integrating these domains into her daily life such that they became inseparable parts of her existence.

When I saw her the second time, we met for coffee at a cafe. She started the conversation abruptly by asking me if I liked Baudelaire. I said no, not especially, and was curious to know why she asked this question. In response, she lit up a slim cigarette, as fashionable European intellectuals tended to do at the time. I must confess, initially, I was not at all impressed by this second meeting with Eliza. I found her manners too conventional, too pretentiously intellectual. I thought that I would be more impressed if she would go ahead and say smart things rather than acting like the kind of person who could say them.

She answered my question by stating that she, herself, adored *The Flowers of Evil*.

Which poems? I asked.

My question seemed to make her uncomfortable. She looked up for a few moments to reflect and exhale a puff of smoke, then answered that, more or less arbitrarily, she would say that the poems about lesbians and indolent cats were her favorites.

I laughed with a cruel little sneer and told her that was really stereotypical.

What was stereotypical? she asked.

Her taste, I replied, growing more and more impatient. I said that it was boring to like the same poems that every person who has artistic pretensions likes. Besides, the fact that she herself was lesbian, made things worse. It made her choice seem even more ordinary and predictable. And as I was saying this, I was also asking myself, was this person, who had seemed so innocent and fresh in the flower shop, a total fake?

Eliza felt insulted. I could sense her anger in the nervous way she put out her cigarette and immediately started smoking another. I was chocking in her smoke and presence. She looked at me and retorted that I had no artistic sensibility. I felt that, as she said this, she blew a mouthful of smoke in my face. Perhaps I was struck only by the impact and insolence of her words.

With this exchange of insults and mutual irritation, our five-year partnership, which was to last until her death and might have never ended, began. It was only the second time we had seen each other and already several barriers had been broken. Retrospectively, I would say that in the course of that conversation, we began to feel vulnerable to each other: not the way strangers do, but the way good friends feel when they care about each other's esteem. We were already resorting to insults, not out of meanness, but out of frankness. For me, that honest anger was a good sign. It meant that we could be open and say what we believed. It meant that tact could be learned and negotiated together, along the way, not carried with us like a shield from the very beginning. But this is how I would frame our relationship today, with hindsight. At the moment I saw things differently. I felt jolted and irritated by that conversation. Had I followed my immediate impulses, I would have left the coffee shop and never seen Eliza again.

For some unknown reason, perhaps inertia, perhaps superficial politeness, perhaps fascination, I stayed. I sat there staring at her, looking hurt and offended. After her own irritation subsided, Eliza acted a little embarassed and started to cough. I caught a glimpse of another facet of her personality, a more open and conciliatory side.

Maybe you're right, she said. But you don't have to put things so harshly. In any case, my favorite poem by Baudelaire doesn't talk about cats or lesbians, or lesbians like cats, or cats like lesbians, and all the rest of what has become commonplace imagery. My favorite poem deals with the subject of good and evil.

As it turns out, her favorite poem by Baudelaire was *To the Reader.* I also liked this poem and wanted to know why she liked it so much. First she said that its soft melody and flow appealed to her. I answered her that one could say that about most of Baudelaire's poems. What was so special about this one?

She looked up, gathered her ideas, then orchestrated them in a sentence with a sweep of her hand. It contrasted with its harshness, with its paradoxical indictment of moralism, she answered making a circular gesture in the air, to dispel all confusion.

Yes, I said, but if the poem indicts moralism, doesn't it do so from an implicitly moralistic stance? Is there such a thing as a non-moralizing judgment?

Not so fast, she replied, making a beseeching gesture, bringing her hands together, the way she would always do from then on when I rushed to judge something, to capture a complex piece of art in a few quick words, or to offer a facile opinion. She asked me to listen more carefully to the poem before rushing to extract its message. To imagine at times that the poem did not even have a message. To think slowly, patiently, with more reverence for its intellectual and artistic beauty.

I told her that I didn't think I had it in me to revere a consecrated artist or piece of art. I was a modern skeptic, I explained.

She begged me to stop attaching labels to everything in sight. She said that I would come to appreciate art if I gave my mind the space and time to perceive it. She said that she agreed with Simone Weil: understanding requires "attention." Not a flexing of muscles in concentration, but a passive overture of mind and body. Not a projection of ready-made ideas, but a total permeability of spirit. Understanding, she said, demands an openness and receptiveness of mind that allows art and thought to penetrate one's being through all its pores; to achieve a miraculous orchestration of all of one's hidden powers of comprehension and sensation.

Then she began reciting the poem from memory, in French. She was almost chanting, pausing at the end of one sequence of rhymes and ideas, then picking up the melody and rhythm of the next. She proceded slowly. Her voice rang, intermingling sweetness and harshness, soothing and torment-ing the ears like the content of her words.

Stupidity, error, sin, meanness
fill up our minds and work upon our bodies,
and we keep our dear pangs of remorse well fed,
as beggars support their vermin.

Our sins are stubborn, our moments of repentance feeble;
we demand a fat reward for our confessions,
and set out cheerfully again on the muddy path,
thinking to wash away all stains with cheap tears.

....
But among the jackals, panthers, hound bitches,
monkeys, scorpions, vultures, snakes,
the yelping, howling, growling, crawling monsters
in the infamous menagerie of our vices,

There is one uglier, wickeder, fouler than all!
He does not strike great attitudes nor utter great cries,
but he would happily lay waste the earth,
and swallow up the world in a yawn.

It is Boredom!--an involuntary tear welling in his eye,
he dreams of scaffolds as he smokes his hookah.
You know him, reader, that fastidious monster--
hypocritical reader, my fellow-man, my brother!

I did not speak for what seemed like a long time after
Eliza had finished reciting the poem. I was waiting for her to
reopen her eyes and did not want to say anything that might
be interpreted as hasty or superficial. So I said nothing,
imitating her. Nevertheless, the poem made me think. I
thought quickly and coherently, in a linear and simple fashion
that she would have undoubtedly scorned.

I thought about what makes people commit evil acts
against other people just out of boredom. I thought tangen-
tially, not so much about the poem itself, as about the ideas
that occured to me as I was listening to it. I thought about the
spectacularity of guilt, about how confessions of wrongdoings
tantalize the listener or viewer. About how complicitous the
processes of telling and listening, or of doing and watching,
are in generating not only a given moral framework, but also
its violation. Often, the one who places himself in the position
of moral judge takes a double pleasure: in listening to the
confession of the "crime" and in judging it as well. I began to
wonder: what do innocence and guilt mean in such a relational
understanding of evil?

They still meant something to me, they meant everything
in fact, and their distinction seemed to be as clear as ever in
my moral scheme. But I could no longer envision that
distinction, formulate it conceptually, or translate it into words.
Baudelaire's poem blocked, without modifying, my ethical
imagination.

Aesthetically, I was a void. My senses were concentrated in a closed sort of way, flexing with tension, with schemes of thought and causal connections of ideas, not with the meditative receptiveness recommended by Eliza. She may have been right. I didn't think much about the beauty of the rhyme of Baudelaire's poem. Its images evoked nothing but rational thought. I reduced not only its poetics, but also its historicity, to a sequence of ideas applicable to contemporary life. For this reason, I always felt like an intellectual dwarf compared to Eliza; I couldn't really fathom her imagination. She was what, for the sake of convenience, I termed a mystic. And like all mystics, she was incomprehensible yet lucid in her own way. I felt drawn to her opaqueness. Perhaps I loved Eliza because in some ways she always eluded me, as much in life as in death.

Despite my sense of mental closure, Eliza's reading helped me appreciate the poetics of life, the beauty of human expression. I thought about her modulated tone and velvety voice; about the way she closed her eyes and breathed more slowly after she had finished reciting the poem; about the way she contemplated it and smoked. The smoke dissipated into raspy tones of her voice; her voice joined the open movements of her arms; her arms fluttered musically to the rhythm of her agitated, active mind. She breathed poetry, in and out, through the pores of her vibrant body. It was as if, after having exhaled the poem through the inflections of her voice, she allowed it to re-enter her slowly, word by word, line by line. She inhaled and exhaled poetry, with a sense of patient hunger and necessity, with an unspeakable adoration.

I felt extraneous to Eliza's intimate process of thought. I was only a voyeur. Like any voyeur, I took pleasure in watching the sensuality of her contemplation, motion and silence. Her face and manner, her hidden and profound intellect, remain imprinted upon my memory like an icon. And if I had to translate her image into a coherent phrase, I would say that Eliza had the most compelling way of refusing to put ideas into words before gestating them slowly, in the womb of her silence.

* * *

Deja vu. My visits to Dr. Herlich always gave me the impression of having already happened. An endless repetition, differentiated only by slight nuances of irritation and pain. The same couch, the same chair, the same knee almost touching my head. But slightly different feelings, modulated sensations, fresh pangs of pain paralyzing my body as I lay stretched out and vulnerable on that impeccably clean white couch.

This time, he said, it has to be different.

What has to be different, I asked.

Your narrative.

You mean my life?

No, he answered. I mean the story of your life, your obsessions, your suffering. You have no power to recount your life, nor does anyone else. All you or other patients can do is recall, interpret and embellish your lives in different ways, from different perspectives. So far, you have only perfected the art of narrating a single event, the one that describing your first meeting with Eliza. It is time to move on; to unravel your former life in all its messiness and contingency.

I felt hermetically sealed to his prodding questions. I told you the truth and have nothing more to say, I answered morosely.

Repression and resistance. That's all you have to offer, he reproached. How do you expect me to help you; how do you expect us to work out your sense of loss, anger and pain?

I don't. I want to be with them forever. They represent the way I can perceive Eliza's absence, the way she remains with me in death.

No, he said surprisingly firmly. Today you will move beyond this impasse. Today you will answer my questions.

Then he paused, perhaps to monitor my physical resistance to his imperatives; to watch with pleasure the mechanical stiffening and closing of my body. I shut my eyes, my fists, my mouth, contracted my muscles, and thus became impenetrable to his words. He began to dissect me, nonetheless, slowly and meticulously, with probing eyes and persistent questions.

How did you find out about Eliza's death?

I was silent.

Who told you that she had died?

Silence again.

How did you find out about Eliza's death? he repeated, calmly, once again.

Eventually, I gave in and told him. I told him that the police called me one day to ask me if I knew a woman by the name of Eliza Russel. I said yes. They asked me if I was this woman's close friend. I said yes. Then they told me, without any further preparation, that Eliza had been murdered. They asked me to come to the station to confirm the indentity of the "victim."

At the time, the word "victim" shocked me even more than the news of Eliza's death. I had never viewed Eliza as a victim; I had always perceived her as a strong, almost indomitable, woman. I felt indescribably sad. Henceforth, she was to be reduced to this pitiful word, to this non-identity, by the murderer, the press, the lawyers, the police, and later, even by myself.

You see, after a while, even I began to adopt the common language and came to regard Eliza as a victim. For me, this word marked the imperceptible moment when Eliza ceased to be alive. The word "victim" evoked the Eliza I saw at the morgue; the Eliza I could barely recognize; the Eliza who could not answer or comfort me when I tried to hold her body as I cried.

It's true, it took me a long time to put the two words, "Eliza" and "victim," together. It took me even longer to put together the words "Eliza" and "death." That particular intersection of words, concepts and mental images was complicated and stupefying beyond belief. How could such a beautiful young woman be dead? Why would anyone want to take Eliza's life? How could a matter of hours separate a glowing, active, and vivacious Eliza from the Eliza they kept calling a victim, body and corpse?

The police did not address any of these questions. They only said that they were sorry. The phone clicked. Then I heard the sound of the dial tone accompanied by a distant voice instructing me to seal Eliza's life with language, to mark her death by uttering her name upon my recognition of her mangled corpse. After all these years together, after all the happiness, the suffering, the turmoil, the ideas, the emotions, and the pleasures that we shared, I had only one role left to play. My final act was to correlate that lifeless, tortured body with Eliza's cherished name.

* * *

Before I met Eliza, sexual relations felt like a kind of oblivion. Both of myself and of the other. It was as if, instead of making me more aware of my bodily existence and desire, the sexual act disembodied me, forcing me to escape into some other, imaginary, realm that only vaguely resembled my experience. For this reason, I tended to resist erotic encounters. If I were sitting at a bar, glancing casually at the people around me, and another woman or even a man looked at me in what seemed to be a sexual way, I would immediately glance elsewhere, turning my head away with an abrupt dismissive motion. All visual conversation was foreclosed before it even began.

It was not out of shyness or prudery that I averted my glance. No. It was more out of a need to form some other kind of intimacy first. At least, this is how I would justify my reaction. Perhaps this response was an anachronistic relic of our cultural past; of the tendency to sever the soul from the body and place the thinking and emotive aspects of human beings above their corporeal desires. At the same time, I resisted quite consciously the opposite, and more recent, cultural trend: of viewing the body and its pleasures as the core of human identity and relations; of having sexual evaluation and desire rule every aspect of my interaction with others. Somehow, I felt the need to coordinate body and mind, to penetrate more fully the intimacy of another being. Perhaps that is why casual encounters intimidated me.

If I did not succeed in discouraging them, if my signs of dismissal were not taken seriously, then I would give in with a sense of resignation that I had to act normal, if only in the minimal sense of having and expressing desire. Without this proof of desire I felt like a vagabond on earth; like a traveler from some other time and space who lacked an identity card. And yet, each time I got my card stamped by having a sexual encounter, each time I made that imaginary and meaningless sign on the bedpost indicating not conquest but mere survival, I felt like I was cheating both society and myself. I may have touched other women, but I never felt them; I may have looked at their beautiful bodies, but only through closed, unreceptive eyes. Sexually, I was like a non-person, neither male nor female, neither gay nor straight.

My encounters always began in similar ways. I would never pursue anyone and only resigned myself to another if her persistence was greater than my resistance. When she would begin talking to me, in the midst of a quiet museum or in the noisy corner of a bar, I would answer curtly yet politely. The conversations moved through me. Words and gestures flowed swiftly from one person to the other, but nothing seemed to happen or connect. My encounter with Ingrid in the museum was typical.

Oh yes, this painting is beautiful, don't you think? Georgia O'Keefe can evoke sensuality through shape and color perhaps better than anyone else.

She has dark eyes and long brown hair. Her long bangs shelter her white forehead, framing the side of her face and giving her a wild-but-tame sexy look.

But how can different styles of painting be compared? So many painters evoked what was considered most sensual for their epoch.

She looks at me a little disappointed. Maybe my short hair and straight figure are a little too boyish for her taste.

Yes, comparison without historical standards becomes an exercise in purely subjective judgment. It translates into saying: I prefer this over that, not into claiming seriously that what I like is most beautiful.

She is certainly beautiful, by all conventional standards. Her black jeans and long white sweater draping her slim and tall body lend her the look of an artist's model. Her makeup is as subtle and trendy as her clothes: brown shades of eyeliner and soft burgundy lipstick complete the look of a perfection you would not allow yourself to touch or kiss for fear of spoiling its artifice. Undoubtedly, she has the perfection of a painting or photograph: a beauty you wish or fail to emulate, not the close warm presence of someone you desire to hold. Her very perfume exudes good taste and distance.

The conversation would then stop prematurely at this meaningless agreement. Then it would resume its course: Do you study art history? she would ask. Again, I would feel inadequate under her glance. Dressed as I was, in blue pants and a red top, I would feel unattractive compared to her.

Oh, no, I know practically nothing about art, I would say. That's really why I come to the museum quite often: not so much to instruct myself but to enjoy looking at the unfamiliar. Why are you here? I would ask in turn.

I study art history at Cleveland State, she replied meaningfully. Then she paused. Was she waiting for me to tell her, in turn, what I did with my life? I did not feel like telling this total stranger anything about myself. What mattered to me would probably be completely indifferent to her. And vice-versa. I would try to respond, out of politeness, nonetheless.

Oh. Lull in the conversation, followed by the polite but uninterested question: What do you study in particular?

Modern painting.

That sounds interesting, I replied as a matter of course. It sounded interesting to me only in a relativistic sense, as much or as little as anything else.

It really is. I learn a lot, especially from my close examination of the paintings themselves. She seemed to look at me for understanding and approval, as if this kind of information provided some hidden clue to herself.

It didn't. I can imagine that is very instructive, I would reply nevertheless. Her own thoughts remained opaque. She seemed more distant, after this meaningless chatter, than when I had first noticed and admired her elegance and beauty from the corner of my eye.

Yes, she continued. The scholarly essays in art history and theory begin to make sense once you actually see the paintings. 'I am an intellectual' she seemed to announce. But our similar education did not create a bond. It simply suggested that, externally, we were manufactured by similar technologies.

That makes a big difference, I concurred. It is less abstract and removed from your own sensory knowledge and experience. I related my education in philosophy to her study of art, found the lowest common denominator between our two fields, and produced the necessary agreement. Would human interaction always be so empty?

It is. Looking at paintings makes all the difference. Pause. Stalling, stalling, there is nothing left to say.

Moving gently, predictably, from one fragment of conversation to another; speaking automatically, with minimal feeling or thought, a stranger and I might, on rare occasions, come to share the same room, the same space, the same bed. Our physical interaction would follow the same predictable flow of our words. Sex would be just one more non-sequitur; one more failure to connect. Nonetheless, our shared desire, reaching the outer limits of pleasure, provided some mutual relief. When we touched in the soft darkness of the room, we no longer felt compelled to talk. Effortless movements would displace belabored words and gestures.

I would touch her face with obligatory tenderness and vacuous eyes. Maybe my eyes communicated depth of feeling, a ripple of emotion that expands the soul only to disappear without a trace. Maybe they did not communicate anything at all. Feeling her skin, tasting her lipstick with increasingly long, penetrating kisses, probing each other's tongues in the long silence of our bodies and minds, would suffice. It was enough of a prelude to the loss of self in titillated and autonomous sensations. My body took over and I was left somewhere far behind, a lost being in small waves of fleeting pleasure. Sometimes it felt good to escape to such an utter lack. I felt free to imagine myself as another, to imagine my partner as someone else. My fantasies were enhanced by the absence of intimacy. I was free to imagine that depth of feeling or understanding were there, in a vague and pleasant form that did not require the effort of any specific elaboration. I was free to envision the outlines of an unrealizable dream, where a nascent love would be gently cradled by the regular folds and movements of sensuality.

* * *

Intimacy craves more intimacy. Until there is no distance left; until you feel like you and your partner share the same breath and exhale at the same moment. The rhythms of our two lives had converged. Nevertheless, I felt like Eliza needed more room to breathe; that she was keeping her distance. She went to classes, to work in a bank, to the gym, all without me. She had her group of friends and I had mine. We never attempted to mix our public lives for fear of mismatch or confusion. Besides, I always felt like her friends were the kind of artistic people who would reject me and that I, in turn, had no real friends to share with her.

It's true here were a few fellow graduate students whom I saw on occasion. We attended the same seminars and discussion groups and, from time to time, we invited each other to chat over lunch or dinner. We dwelled obsessively on professional subjects: this or that school of thought, the uncertainty of our professional futures, social or philosophical currents which might have touched the hidden corners of our lives. But out of this professional chatter and gossip, no friendship ever emerged. In fact, it seemed like just the opposite took place. The more we divulged our personal lives, the more we had reasons to envy or reject each other; to expose each other's vulnerabilities while being critical of the fact that they were being openly displayed. I could not call these colleagues friends, even measured by very cynical standards of friendship. The most I could do was to view these acquaintanceships as human relations that disciplined me into a reluctant and cold sociability.

The more I felt distanced from other people, the more I grew attached to Eliza. I became concerned about the fact that we were spending so little time together; that there were so few moments to share during the course of a busy day. I grew jealous of Eliza's friends and possessive about her time.

Why did she see *Piano* without me when she knew how much I wanted to see it together? How could she make time to have lunch with other friends, but not to eat dinner with me, as any other couple would?

I started nagging Eliza about the clutter in her life. She was always on the run, from one event to another, from one person to another. I felt expelled by the centrifuge of her energetic existence; pushed off somewhere toward the far borders of her active life. I began to fear being replaced or forgotten. I alternated between hating myself and chastizing her.

What qualities did I have, other than my great need and attachment to Eliza, to make her stay with me forever? I rarely posed the opposite question. It seemed obvious to me that Eliza had so many qualities that I could never envision leaving or forgetting her. I always reviewed her virtues in my mind, comparing her favorably to every other human being I had met. She was sensitive, intelligent, ethical and compassionate, I would say to myself. Could she say the same thing about me? Most likely not.

Following this train of thought, my obsession became: how could I convince or somehow trick Eliza into loving me forever? I insisted on the concept of forever. I needed that abstract reassurance that I would never be left to fight alone the battle of life on this earth. I asked for guarantees: Will you always love me?

She would never answer in the banal, usual way: yes, of course. She would tell me exactly what she thought. She said that she cared about me enormously, yes, that she even loved me, but that she could not promise me any false certainties in life. To promise to love me forever would be a possible lie. She simply did not know if our feelings would last; if our lives and emotions would remain as static as a simple promise of love.

But, I would persist, lives don't have to be static for love to evolve, to continue forever, until death do us part, as they say.

Until death do us part, she would repeat with an ironic smile. She was amused by my allusion to marriage and told me that we could not rely upon the same certainties as "them." "Us" and "them" were Eliza's favorite codewords whenever the issue of marriage came up.

According to Eliza, "they" were the people who had hundreds of years of convention to guide their actions. We, on the other hand, were the people who had to manufacture our lives from a bric-a-brac of contradictory norms and desires; we were the builders of a new kind of relationship with tenuous foundations and an uncertain fate.

I often criticized her way of placing us on the margins of society. It seemed like a way of indicting our behavior compared to more conventional relationships. But she always responded that she did not mean to judge our lives as morally better or worse: only to note that, because of the way society functioned at the moment, our lives were less reliant upon those institutions, such as marriage, that attempted to create a sense of stability in social life.

Aware of her opinions and resistance to conventions, I nonetheless continued urging her to increase her commitment. But my persistence only irritated her. I even went so far as to buy her an engagement ring and ask her to marry me. Predictably, she refused. I felt enormously hurt. To me, her cautious words only indicated that she did not love me as much as I loved her. Perhaps I was wrong. Perhaps I lacked the generosity of spirit to interpret her honesty as a sign of different values; as something that does not directly relate to me at all. Perhaps I chose not to understand her.

In desperation, I came up with another impossible idea: why not adopt or have a child together? A child would unify us; it would create a common genealogy even if we could not both be her biological parents. Eliza marvelled at what she called the vulgarity of my ideas.

She asked me point blank: was conventional life all I longed for? Were marriage and children my most important goals in life? If yes, then why choose to live with her rather than with a man?

I was equally stunned by her thinking: Could I not love a woman the way other women love men? What was wrong with that? Were we not human; did we not have desires and emotions; could we not long for stability and continuity, just like everyone else?

No, she answered. Not like everyone else.

It is true that Eliza did not have many conventional desires. She wanted to leave her life open-ended; to allow space for discovery and change; to seal her life with no irrevocable promises or plans.

I, on the other hand, needed more security from her. All other aspects of my existence were uncertain: whether or not my parents would reject me was a source of anxiety; whether or not I would ever find a stable job was a great uncertainty; whether or not I would ever believe in friendship remained a cynical and pointless question. I demanded, with an increasing sense of urgency, only one certainty from life: Eliza's love.

* * *

As far as I can recall, the trial was not meant to establish the man's innocence or guilt. No. The evidence was overwhelming. What was at stake, what was to be determined and negotiated in court, was the precise nature and extent of the murderer's innocence and guilt. I went to trial hoping to help persuade the jury that the man who killed Eliza epitomized a cowardly, banal, but also very real and threatening human evil. I wanted to lend support to the argument that he killed for his own pleasure; that he did not have the ethical strength to imagine himself in his victim's position; that he took pleasure in the irreversibility of their roles.

I never thought of this man as a monster, though I did think that his actions could be regarded as monstrous. When I looked at him, when I heard his voice, those incoherent words of explanation and defense, I thought that he was only human. Human, yes, but in a minimal sort of way: he had a human shape and experienced fear and self-love. Human also in a frightening sort of way, that, in my opinion, was more destructive than a vicious animal, poisonous plant, or any other living being.

The prosecutor tried to convince the jury that this man was sane and evil. The defense insisted that he was insane and only human. By the end of the trial, the jury appeared somewhat confused about the boundaries between sanity and insanity delineated by this horrible act. They wavered, deliberated many times, then finally agreed upon a verdict as arbitrary as the toss of a coin. What else can one do when confronted with the limits of the comprehensible?

Perhaps the jury was moved by the man's tears, flowing liberally and self-indulgently upon his rotund face. Somehow, the tears seemed to flow from his baldness, emanate from his cheeks, blend into the moistness of his puffy hands. He said many things, sometimes coldly and dispassionately, at other times excited and sobbing for no apparent reason.

He said that he loved Eliza as a mother. When asked why, he answered that he found her gait cruel and maternal.

He said that she had tempted him when walking down the street. When asked how, he said because she was female and wore black.

He said that he was very unhappy. When asked when, he could not differentiate the present from the future or the past. His answer was timeless: forever.

He said that he felt horrible. When asked why, he said because he was labeled a criminal, a rapist and a murderer, and these words lacerated him, wounded his sensibilities, stuck to his body and tore his flesh while he tried to escape into a safer world.

They asked him if he felt pity and remorse. He answered yes, he did. For whom, they asked. For himself.

Psychiatrists were brought in to translate his utterances, to explain the implications of his words. After their explanations, his words seemed more incomprehensible, and certaintly more contradictory, than ever.

The psychiatrists brought by the defense argued that his answers were clearly incoherent, the symptoms of a mentally ill mind. This man was not conscious of the evil he committed. He could barely differentiate hallucinations from real people, Eliza from the mother who abused him during childhood, the present from the past. His world was populated by nightmares, nightmares we could not even begin to imagine. He deserved pity, not punishment; help, not rejection. The only just thing to do, the defense maintained, would be to find him not guilty of first degree murder and recommend treatment in a mental institution.

The psychiatrists brought by the prosecution argued that this man epitomized conscious evil. He was not a traumatized victim, but a clever actor. He simulated the symptoms of a mentally ill man with exquisite skill. He was aware of the crime he commited and would take pleasure in getting away with it. There was no evidence that he had been abused as a child, but blaming all your problems on child abuse, and particularly on abusive women, was a familiar mysogynist defense for criminal acts. Nothing could justify what he had done to Eliza Russel. The real nightmare was not in his mind, but in his action. He was a monster: a sane, evil, destructive, and selfish being who obviously only thought of the effect of the crime on him and never felt pity or remorse for the victim. The only just sentence, the prosecution argued, would be to convict him of first-degree murder.

I was torn between these two explanations, neither of which seemed to match either the deed or the man. The act was clear but the actor was impenetrable. His contradictory identities were constructed right then and there, before our eyes, in order to substantiate different moral claims. He became the major premise of a syllogism: if he was taken as sane, then his act was a crime; if he was interpreted as insane, then his act was not a crime. Only the minor premise, that he had killed Eliza, was never questioned.

In my own mind, I constructed a different kind of identity for this man. I did not care if he were sane or insane. In fact, his psychological, personal or sociological histories did not matter to me at all. The only thing that counted was precisely the minor premise taken for granted by everyone else: if he killed Eliza, not why he did it. Asking why was giving a man who was so bestial a humane face. I wished the trial would allow for a more existentialist kind of justice: one that links man and act without giving him extra masks, extra hypothetical or real identities, extra layers of protection and subterfuge, lines of defense to which the victim had no recourse when she was lying naked, terrified and vulnerable; when she was pleading for her life before him.

Above all, I wished the jury would realize that this man was mean but not monstrous. I believed that the prosecution was giving him too much credit in mythologizing him as a monster; that the defense was giving him too much credit in mythologizing his past suffering as the stuff that fashions monstrosity. It seemed that the whole trial was, perversely, an ode to this man's evil, viewed either as a monstrosity of being (by the prosecution) or as a monstrosity of social or psychological development (by the defense). Either way, the killer was not regarded as what I believed him to be: an opportunistic, crafty "human being" who might not have been sane, but certainly knew what he was doing and how to cover up what he had done. The whole trial became an extended parenthesis, a long elaboration of popular wisdom about the nature of criminals and crime, rather than an examination of what this man had done and what should be done to him in turn.

After a few hours of interrogation of witnesses, experts, doctors and police, I got a sense of the classification of pertinent issues and questions. The least relevant questions were: Did this man have a record of violent crime against women? Did this man torture, rape and kill Eliza? Did this man commit such a horrific crime deliberately, with full knowledge of what he was doing? Did Eliza deserve the right to live beyond the age of 23? Did this man have a right to kill Eliza?

The most relevant questions were: Did Eliza have a record of promiscuous sexual behavior? Objection. Was Eliza dressed in a provocative manner? Objection. Was Eliza homosexual? Objection. Had she been previously involved with or provoked the criminal in any way? No.

The most highly debated questions were: What was sanity? Could any man who tortured and killed women be called sane, or should all such men be considered insane? Should violent crimes be excused in the name of insanity? Should violent criminals deserve the opportunity to reform, to become fully human, to live?

If I understood correctly, on balance, what mattered most was not that Eliza had been found raped and murdered at the age of twenty-three. No. What mattered most was that the thirty-eight year old man who had taken her life had a right to live.

The man was found not guilty of second-degree murder by reason of insanity and was subsequently commited to a mental institution. Upon the recommendation of psychiatrists, he could be allowed to go free, and perhaps kill other women, whenever the doctors deemed him to be sane. According to double jeopardy, he could never be re-tried and punished for Eliza's murder because he had already been found not guilty of a crime it was generally acknowledged that he had committed.

The medical rationale for such a sentence went as follows. The psychiatrists brought by the defense, who were the ones who were eventually believed by the jury, testified that the man was clinically insane. They even endowed him with a new identity: he was no longer a criminal, but a paranoid schizophrenic. Because he was mentally dysfunctional, he could not be held responsible for his crime. His mental condition justified his hospitalization, but not for life, since paranoid schizophrenia is treatable by therapy and anti-psychotic medication. If the patient took underwent treatment, the logic went, he could be expected to function as a "normal" human being within a relatively short period of time. According to privacy and confidentiality laws, no one would know of this man's criminal record once he assumed his new identity: the identity of a "normal man."

The ethical rationale for the sentence observed a different logic. Since it was too late to bring Eliza back to life anyway, why claim yet another human life and perpetuate the chain of murders? Furthermore, if statistics "proved" that criminals did not take the death penalty as a disincentive for committing crimes, why should the state set a bad example by committing murder in the name of justice? Besides, from a theological perspective, what gives the state the right to play the role of God by taking human lives?

These series of questions and answers heated the entire courtroom. Everyone was up in arms about them; everyone seemed to care. Not I. For me, such ethical nuances had become meaningless. I did not care about the right to life of the man who took upon himself the right to take Eliza's life. In my opinion, he had given up all of his rights, every freedom and responsibility that his supposed humanity entailed, in taking an innocent person's life. He proved himself neither inhuman nor superhuman, but, quite simply, a bad human.

I did not consider this issue abstractly from the perspective of either consequentialist or universalist justice. No. For me, the question of crime and punishment was posed in a much more personal way. This question, which was really more of an answer, had two faces attached to it: Eliza's on one side and the criminal's on the other. These two mental images did not symbolize good and evil or any other popular polarization. It seemed irrelevant and misleading to try to describe Eliza as a saint--why should she have been one?--and the criminal as a monster--why should he be given so much credit? Instead, these two mental images represented a violent encounter between two human beings in which one effectively and unilaterally destroyed the humanity of the other for no comprehensible or defensible reason. In light of this double image, my rhetorical question became: How can this man, this overweight man with disheveled brown hair and dark eyes; this man who had raped two women and murdered one of them; this man who committed horrible crimes but was declared innocent, be eliminated, once and for all, from the face of the earth?

* * *

Eliza, they say that victims are always cold.
And yet each night I feel your warm touch,
Palpating my skin, softly and lightly,
With the tenderness of a caressing hand.
Eliza, they say that victims are always silent.
And yet each day I hear your familiar voice,

Brushing my ears, softly and lightly,
With the regular beat of a pulsating heart.
Eliza, they say that victims are always motionless.
And yet each night I feel you roaming within me,
Arousing my memories, softly and lightly,
With the tantalizing sweep of a delicate breeze.
Eliza, they say that victims are always absent.
And yet each day I sense your fleeting presence,
Eluding my grasp, softly and lightly,
With the haughty carelessness of a living ghost.
You may be cold, and silent,
and motionless, and absent, Eliza,
But you are still the warmth I long for in the coldness of
my nights,
The voice I strain to hear during waking hours,
The force that moves me
and the presence that haunts me night and day,
and day and night again.
Would you have believed it Eliza?
They say that victims don't count.
They don't see, they don't speak, they don't feel, they
don't breathe:
They don't count.
Or at least, they say that you count
Only in a statistical sort of way,
Where your lives and your deaths do not matter at all.
Despite what they say,
Would you believe it Eliza?
I continue to live, think and speak only to understand
why.
Why they say that your life has no meaning
Just because someone decided to take it away.
Why they say that your life has no meaning,
Just because you had not acquired money or fame.
Why they say that your life has no meaning,
Just because human life is microscopically small.
Why they say that in the bigger scheme of things, Eliza,
Our lives hardly matter at all.
You were just a speck of dust from a cosmic perspective,
A little ant from an earthly perspective,
An unknown woman from a human perspective,
A piece of mortified flesh from the murderer's perspective,

And everything that mattered on earth from my
perspective.
I link up the logic of the order of things
And still cannot explain to you why.
Why in this world,
With its chaotic order of meaning and significance,
Should my perspective,
And your life,
Always come last.

* * *

Tell me a little bit about what you *didn't* like about Eliza.
The same couch, the same chair, the same man, the same
uncomfortable circumstances.
Why would I want to do that? I asked him puzzled.
Because, he answered, it seems to me like you idealize
Eliza in order to idealize yourself.
I don't understand.
There seems to have been nothing wrong with your
relationship, at least the way you have described it to me so
far. It was without problems, fights, or tensions. It was flawless:
a relationship between two perfect beings, not a human bond.
In all the sessions we have had so far, you have told me so
little about you and Eliza as real people.
I did not come here to desecrate Eliza's memory to a
perfect stranger, I answered abruptly.
I realize that. But you came to talk about your life
together and you have been too selective about what you have
told me. I don't feel at all ready to evaluate your condition.
Aside from being aware of your reticence to talk about your
life with Eliza and knowing the source of your pain, I know
very little about you. How do you feel right now?
I turned around and looked at him open-eyed: I feel
dismayed. I don't know how to answer you. He waited
patiently, so I pursued my chain of thought. I mean, you
expect me to open myself up to you like a body on the
dissecting table. But even bodies don't open themselves up,
just like that, of their own accord. The doctors do all the work.
He paused to reflect for a moment, then asked: Would you
be open to hypnosis as part of your treatment?

I'm not sure, I replied. I feel like hypnosis would be an easy way out for you: a way of getting me to answer your questions in spite of myself.

Yes, to some extent it would. Although, by the same token, hypnosis cannot force you to do something that is completely against your will. It just weakens your resistance to analysis and makes the process of talking about your past less painful.

I hesitated before answering, but finally agreed to try hypnosis. More for him than for myself. To placate him a little; to make him think that his treatment was beginning to work. To fool him?

* * *

I started to write to him as if I were a stranger. A stranger drawn to his actions, to his confused feelings and perceptions of women, to his crime itself. Sometimes I would underline significant words and phrases in his letters of response; at other times I would take notes as if I were his apprentice. In a sense I was. I tried to learn his craft, his way of dissolving human life along with the sense of responsibility for that dissolution. I copied the phrase "Women want to turn you on and then leave you." Each word made sense, but the meaning of the whole sentence seemed obscure. Which women? How does he know our desires? When does he give us a chance to live? Is the "you" male or female? Would that make any difference? I circled all the insulting epithets, trying to rummage deep through the trash of his mind. Bitches, whores, angry words without definite reason or direction, populated his imaginary feminine world. Could I train myself to think similarly about men? Thinking of him made it easy: if I could convince myself that all men were like him, that mankind was a universal rather than a series of particulars, then I could easily see how they are all bastards and assholes. Was this process of generalization convincing? Not yet. I had more to learn from a mind that was saturated with hatred.

I would respond to his letters regularly, with increasing frequency and sensitivity, trying to pry open the innermost parts of his being with the violent sensation that I was cracking open his skull. At times he seemed flattered by my unwavering attention. He once confessed that he liked me so much, that if he met me, he would instantly kill me. How? I asked.

In his next letter, he ignored my question and complained of poor nutrition in the institution. So I changed my strategy and stopped asking him how. I asked why. I told him that I would bring him food to the hospital if he would tell me why he killed women.

For a long time, he did not respond. I thought I lost contact with him: I moved too fast; I wanted to know too much. Eventually, however, after a period of two months, he answered. His letter was a long shopping list: sausage, swiss cheese, wheat bread, honey, cereal, peanut butter, jam, beef jerky, sweets.

I did not reply. When he wrote me again, he said that if I didn't bring the food, when he got out he would kill me. I answered that I would not give him anything other than myself. Then I went to visit him at the hospital. I was not the same person who had gone to his trial, but a smaller, thinner, effaced person with shorter hair, glasses and finer features. I had changed. Both inside and out.

When he first saw me, he smiled. But only briefly, from a distance. He did not approach me; he even turned away. I did not approach him either. I just looked at him casually, as if he were the least interesting feature of the hospital room. A white bed, tan walls, a wooden table and chair, an open closet with a few dark clothes, two lamps, two hospital officials, and him. Those were the objects in his room.

Did you bring the food? he asked.

I did better than that, I said. I brought myself.

What can you mean to me? he sneered. Less than nothing at all.

That's why I'm important, I replied. I have come to help you understand how a human being can mean nothing at all.

Because you did not bring me the food, that's why! He got angry, like a child, almost to the point of tears.

Tell me, I asked, what did you think when you were writing to me? What did you think about my letters?

Not much. I thought that you could be useful; that you could get for me some things I needed. I thought that your letters were annoying and couldn't understand why you wanted to write me. He laughed, then continued to say: But all that didn't really matter. I didn't attach a body or face to your letters. You weren't a woman to me.

Am I a woman to you now? I asked.

He looked me over, or rather looked over me, with the same air of casual disdain I had when I first glanced at him.

No. You are not a woman to me and you will probably never be one.

Why?

He shook his head. Because I already know something about you. Not much, but even a little can spoil everything. You might as well be a man.

Would you ask a man to bring you food and then threaten to kill him if he didn't do it?

He considered the question, then answered, quite firmly: No, not unless I were starving. I did that to you because I did not consider you a man.

Then what am I?

A possible source of food, he answered with a smile.

And how do you think I feel about you?

I don't care.

Then why do you respond to my letters?

He looked at me with empty eyes. Because I'm bored.

I was starting to understand this man. He was a force more than a being: a pure centripetal motion, spinning everything around him to direct it inside. If something he spun around shattered to pieces, he didn't care, even if that something was human flesh. To him, subjects and objects were the same; what mattered was his all-devouring sense of satisfaction.

I told him that I felt sorry for him having to put up with bad hospital food. I said that I would bring him the food he asked for if he could obtain permission to receive it. He looked at the hospital officials. They said that it all depended upon the nature of our relationship. I said I was his cousin and he backed up my lie. They said they didn't know. I looked at him and promised to try.

After I left, we continued our chain of empty correspondance. But everything had changed. I felt that there was nothing more to say or comprehend. It's not that I had understood every aspect of his being, but that I understood enough to know that I was not interested in exploring any further. Nevertheless, I went through all the motions as before, even though by then I knew that all these letters were as meaningless to him as they became to me.

I visited him many times, always posing as his cousin. I came at Thanksgiving, Christmas, Easter, his birthday. Each time I would try to bring him some kind of gift: a new toothbrush, books, a few articles of clothing. He liked the chocolate candy. He had a terrible weakness for sweets. I also eventually brought him the food he had asked for, but much later, so that he would not think that I feared him. In fact, that was the truth. I saw that this predatory killer was only was a fat man trying to grow even larger by consuming the world. I came to visit him on the fourth of July, but the hospital officials informed me that he had suddenly died. They did not explain why and I did not ask. I can only speculate that, given his careless overeating, he must have died of food poisoning.

* * *

I remember the first time that Eliza and I made love. It was an unexpected yet vaguely longed for event, as was my first encounter with Eliza. It seemed like we had waited forever to explore each other's bodies in the same way that we explored each other's minds. Not that our relationship was passionless; in fact, it was the strength of our desire that gave us the patience to wait. Wait for what? Even we were not sure. Neither of us believed that the body was the last thing to be shared with another, even if both of us might have thought that it was not the first thing either. Still, we waited together for nothing at all. We lived as housemates for six months, not daring to cross paths in the bathroom, knocking cautiously on each other's bedroom doors before entering. At times I thought that we kept our distance because we were afraid to ruin everything. What if passion would make us change our minds, evaluate each other harshly, and jeopardize the delicate friendship we had formed? At other times, I thought that our distance was more intuitive and physical than consciously intellectual. Even while feeling attracted, our bodies repelled each other with an instinctive sense of caution and fear of touch. The longer we waited for something to happen, the more we got used to being together while remaining apart.

One day, I entered our living room, tired as usual from attending classes and teaching all day. In the meager glimmer of light offered by the tv screen, the first thing I saw was Eliza's face moistened by tears. I felt a pang of pain and anxiety without even suspecting the cause of her sadness. What is the matter Eliza? I asked. She was sobbing so violently, that she lacked the strength to share her thoughts.

She shook and I held her and she cried and I felt overwhelmed by the waves of sadness and tears. Neither of us knew what to do or say. Abruptly, with mechanical movements, Eliza got up from the couch and went to her room. She was obviously too upset to talk. But how could I help her without even knowing what was wrong? I waited a few minutes, listened to the silent echoes of the house, then attempted to talk to Eliza. When I knocked on her door, she did not reply. I entered the room very slowly, like an intruder. Eliza was no longer crying. Nevertheless, her body continued to shake silently, emptied of the flow of tears, but not of its currents of pain. She was lying on her bed in the dark, looking up at the ceiling, with her thin arms wrapped around her body as if trying desperately to contain its explosive emotions.

I went to the bed, sat on its edge, feeling uncertain about what I should do. Looking at Eliza's corpse-like figure filled me with compassion. I gently placed my hand on her forehead, not clinically like a doctor, but tenderly like a lover and friend. Then I wrapped her cold hands in my own and warmed them with my breath and kisses. I stretched my whole body next to hers to provide her with extra warmth and security, she who felt so despairingly lonely and cold.

Eventually, her body stopped shaking, although I could not tell why, how and when. All I knew was that at some moment I felt a warm, revived and softer body next to mine. I kissed Eliza like a mother would a child and she returned my affection with a voracious, needy kiss. She looked at me and her moist eyes glimmered like silent mirrors, reflecting back all her vulnerability and pain. I stroked her hair, her breasts, her legs, gently touching not her body, but her clothes, as if to add an extra layer of protection against the world, against my own desire. I was afraid of getting too close, of upsetting her further.

But it was she who allayed my fears. She removed my clothes and her own with a sense of impulsive hunger for human contact. Each time I touched her thin naked body, each time her hands caressed my own, I felt myself become lost in a poignant sensitivity that intermingled pleasure and pain; that tempered the force of desire in waves of compassion for her unspeakable fragility.

* * *

A few days later, I still did not dare ask Eliza what was wrong. I could not see how my knowing the source of her pain would help her. Disclosing one's vulnerabilities to another reinforces what might have been a fleeting pain. One day, however, when we were just sitting and talking about other events, she answered, all of a sudden, my unspoken question. She turned toward me, looked me straight in the eyes with unsuspected strength, and told me that I would not be able to understand her without understanding her suffering.

Why did she suffer? I finally asked.

She told me that her suffering was impersonal. Sometimes the pain of the world would simply overwhelm her, merge with her own memories and emotions, and shake up her being in torrents of unhappiness. She had cried a few days ago because so many mass graves had been discovered in Bosnia. She had cried because simple-minded hatred and cruelty could lead human beings to exterminate their own kind and to eventually enjoy the process of destruction in itself, without any additional justifications. She cried, above all, she explained, because the seeds of destruction were as arbitrary as the seeds of compassion. A few days ago she had been overwhelmed by emotion; yesterday she had watched the news about the ethnic cleansing in Bosnia while eating and enjoying her dinner. Yesterday, she insisted, she had not cried. She felt as puzzled by her own reaction as by the violence itself. It was not that she and the killers were equally culpable, she explained, but that it was equally incomprehensible that human beings could commit and learn to accept mass murder as an ordinary event; as an understandable set of acts that could be analyzed and rationalized in terms of complex historical, ethnic and religious rivalries. What if these rivalries were only an epiphenomenon? she asked. What if the real root of murder was--and here she paused, as if dismayed by her own conclusion--well, simply, that humans were at base violent and evil in that way?

I said, yes, I understand, then asked her the usual questions: why did she need to think and suffer about all that? Was not her very suffering a luxury; should she not be happy to be alive, relatively wealthy, living in America?

Then she asked me in turn, if people like her did not care about the Bosnians, then who would?

I responded, somewhat insensitively, that even if people like her did care--that is, if they cared whenever sadness accumulated within them--even then, so what?

She answered with conviction and passion. So this: Sympathy makes horrific events appear in the proper perspective: as unacceptable, unimaginable, and incomprehensible. It makes such events invade our daily conscience and consciousness, such that even people like her, with no special resources, knowledge, or skills, could occassionally care about the plight Bosnian or Somalian women and men. That is all it can do, she concluded in a reserved tone. Sympathy develops us into minimally ethical, not only violent and insensitive, beings.

So that we can continue to enjoy our comfortable lives and do nothing about it? I asked.

Perhaps, she replied. But in any case, she explained, so that we could feel suffering and compassion, hatred and pain, sense of wrong and desire for healing, not only violence. So that we can continue to try, even if we fail, to be only human. Did I understand what she meant?

I only wish I had.

* * *

I lay down and told him, quite calmly, that I had changed my mind about undergoing hypnosis.

Why, he asked me, dismayed. That might have been your best chance of improving.

I know. But I don't feel ready to relinquish control over my mind yet. I have to know and trust you more.

He seemed to accept my answer but persisted: Would you be willing to talk with me more freely without hypnosis? he asked.

Out of anxiety about what I might say during hypnosis, I said yes. I told him that I would be willing to talk to him about the more painful moments of my life with Eliza.

His next question surprised me. How about Isabella? he asked. I thought that I had never mentioned Isabella to him.

I would talk about Isabella later, I told him. First I have to be able to describe what really matters to me.

His tone disapproved. You mean to suggest that Isabella doesn't matter to you?

No, I explained, I wouldn't put it quite so harshly. I mean to say that Isabella cannot matter to me meaningfully without my overcoming my sense of loss for Eliza.

He changed the subject once again. What was Eliza like? I mean, not only what is she like now, when you idealize her because you lost her, but give me some idea what she was really like.

It is difficult to give you a total picture of a person, I answered. Identity is made up of so many incongruous, kaleidoscopic fragments. All one can see is different facets of them, and even those, colored by one's own perception. Last time you gave me a more specific request, I added, one which I believe I am more prepared to answer. You told me to round out the description of my relationship with Eliza by recounting some of our difficult moments. I can talk about that, if you wish, but I still don't understand why you ask me to do it.

He answered calmly: Because I feel like your unhealthy process of mourning, which prevents you from continuing a normal life, is nurtured by an idealization of your past with Eliza. I'm not asking you to criticize Eliza: only to see her closer to the way you saw her when she was alive.

I felt confused by his request. It is not that I did not understand or agree with his judgment; I just did not know where to begin the description. I felt like I was being asked to become something of a fiction writer; to transform my memories of Eliza into a "realistic" character and plot. This was a very difficult process, since what seemed true-to-life to me had seemed too idealized to my psychiatrist, a man who had become the audience of my life-as-art. For the moment, I rejected the role of the meticulous author. I began my new story at a random moment that flashed through my mind, without any particular sense or order.

The incidents of the toothbrushes really bothered me, I said, and then kind of chuckled to myself.

Dr. Herlich seemed confused. What do you mean?

I mean that Eliza had this mania of keeping everything clean and our hygienic habits entirely separate. I could not use her soap, her shampoo, her comb or her make-up. I asked her why all the time. Why the soap or shampoo, if germs could not be transmitted by sharing them? Out of discipline, she would reply.

But we kiss and share germs all the time, I would object.

She just answered, that's different. One sharing was about desire and feelings, the other was about personal cleanliness. She refused to mix the former with the latter.

What did her attitude indicate to you? he interjected.

It made me uncomfortable sometimes. It made me read her mania for cleanliness as a symptom of her desire to keep a distance between us. We were together, and yet, she seemed to indicate that we could never really share the most intimate aspects of ourselves.

But why did you feel the need to unite with her so completely; to deprive her of her personal habits and space?

His question surprised me. I thought that he would deem Eliza's action abnormal; instead, this is how he judged my own. By putting me on the defensive, by acting like he was on her side, was he attempting to distance me from Eliza? Was he trying to get me to criticize the woman I loved so that I myself would appear normal? What cowardice that would take! I resisted the impulse of self-defense and simply inculpated myself. Yes, I replied. I was always insecure about losing Eliza.

Why?

Perhaps because she was the first person I loved aside from family members. I had tried to find someone like her for a long time, and once I found her, I was afraid to lose her.

But why would you lose her if the two of you were so much in love?

Because, as she often said, you can fall out of love; circumstances and people can change, and anything can happen to separate two people who once felt intimately close.

Did you ever think that you might be the one who would decide to end the relationship?

No, never. I was always afraid of losing Eliza, never afraid that she might lose me.

Why?

Because I felt that I found in Eliza someone better than myself yet at the same time someone who was just perfect for me. We understood each other in a way that no one else could relate to either of us. We were a good match.

Did Eliza share your opinion?

I'm not sure that I knew what Eliza felt or thought about me: it was one aspect of our lives which we did not discuss. We talked about our families, our sexual orientation, social or political issues, school and philosophical issues, but not ourselves. It seemed like "us" conversations would get us into trouble.

In what way?

They would make us focus on the negative--what is wrong with "us", why homosexual relations cannot work in a predominantly heterosexual society, why we weren't right for each other--instead of just living and enjoying our lives. "Us" conversations only occured when we had problems. They never took place when we felt good about life.

Was that because you were afraid to plan for your future?

I was surprised by his perceptiveness. Yes, I answered, it was because in some ways we had to live day by day. We could not even tell our parents that we were gay because we were both afraid of causing family crises. We just told them we were best friends and housemates.

Did they suspect anything?

I don't think they wanted to suspect anything. They closed their eyes in order to spare themselves suspicion, judgment and pain. They wanted to believe that we were both adjusted, independent women who were just too studious to marry young.

What makes you say that you were not adjusted?

Speaking for myself, I feel that it is difficult to adjust or lead a normal life when your alternative is to either "come out," traumatize your family and be judged by many as immoral or abnormal, or to live a secret life and pretend that you are like the majority of people.

He pursued his line of questioning: Did Eliza feel that her homosexuality made her life as...difficult... as it made yours?

No. I think that Eliza thought in a more European way. She had lived in Paris for a few years. She told me that she really liked the fact that in Paris people did not air their dirty laundry in public. "Airing dirty laundry" was her favorite expression to describe any kind of social complaining about discrimination or disadvantage. The way she viewed it, if she was gay that was only her business and mine. It was an entirely private taste, analogous to preferring taking baths to showers. What I mean to say is that for her sexual orientation was not only a private matter, but also in many ways an insignificant one. It did not have resounding implications for all other areas of life.

But you just told me that she was afraid to tell her family about you.

Yes, but not exactly for the same reason I hesitated to tell mine. She did not tell her family because she thought that it was none of their business. There are many personal details one does not share with one's family; for her, sexuality was one of them. For me, the opposite was true, at least until Eliza died. When I lived with her, I felt that sexuality defined my identity: meaning both my gender as a woman and my sexual orientation as a lesbian. I tended to view these two facts as shaping almost every aspect of my private and public interactions.

How did it do that?

What can I tell you? In every way. It determined whom I loved, what I told about myself to others, the lies I had to invent about my nonexistent boyfriends to family and friends, my sense of distance from men, everything.

That's interesting that you say your "sense of distance from men." Does that mean that you disliked men even before Eliza's murder?

No, and I wouldn't say that I dislike all men even now. I like some people; I dislike others: all this, regardless of their gender. In any case, I corrected him, I didn't say my dislike for men, but my distance from them. My closest friends, especially when I was young, have always been women. Men are in some ways strangers to me.

But if you did not even have relations with men, then how can you tell for sure that you are not attracted to them?

I didn't mean to say that I had no relations with men. Just that they were not close. I experimented with having boyfriends at some point. Actually, during my teenage years I didn't view dating boys as an experiment, but as a normal experience. It just didn't seem to arouse anything in me: desire, love, caring, attachment. Nothing.

Maybe you hadn't found the right man? Dr. Herlich asked.

Maybe I'm not the right kind of woman, I replied.

Do you regret delimiting and labeling your identity?

No, I replied, glancing at my watch and getting up from the couch, since my hour was over. Then I looked him in the eyes and asked him point blank: Do you?

* * *

His death settled within me, giving me a glimmer of happiness and peace of mind. If only for a day, I caught a glimpse of the spring sun, radiant and enveloping in its tenderness and warmth, and the sky seemed bluer than ever before. I returned to the park where I used to walk and jog with Eliza. A light breeze gently brushed my short hair, caressing and soothing my body and mind. I walked around the sunny park with a sense of freedom in my step. I could not help responding to the world around me, a world of sunshine, chirping birds, flowers and trees, parents and children, a beautiful world I had regarded as dead. As I walked along a narrow sidewalk, a little puppy came close, cautiously smelled my feet and allowed me to touch its little head. I smiled and caressed its velvety body. I loved the feel of its fur, the sense of its vulnerability, trusting affection and fragile life. When he went away, I could not help but feel a sense of loss. I had come into close contact with a warm fragment of life; I had formed an ephemeral attachment. I felt happy.

Elated, I sat down on a bench, trying to absorb the energy and sunshine around me. Closing my eyes, I withdrew into myself and perceived a kaleidoscope of beautiful colors. Red and purple blended with orange and black and danced together in my imagination. A symphony of voices accompanied this vision. I heard the happy voices of children, screaming with the thrill of playful excitement. I heard the cautioning voices of adults, tempering the atmosphere with their lower tones. I even thought I heard the silent whispers of lovers protecting their intimacy with a furtive caress. And when all this sound, color and motion permeated my being, I felt lost in the small yet magnificent universe which had become my world. For the first time since Eliza's death, I could not separate myself from the world and the world from myself. Concentrated in an invisible point in the universe, we were both boundless and eternal.

* * *

After returning from the park, still luminous with peace and happiness, I went back to my room and passed Isabella without even saying hello. She had learned to ignore all of my fleeting moods, the signs of a splintered and tortured personality. When I entered my room, I had a vague sense that someone had followed me home. I remembered a shadow in the park, a shadow that erased the imprints of my momentary joy. I only wished I could have turned around, become aware of it at the moment when I lost my guard and allowed the world to infiltrate me as the warm sunshine penetrates gently and intangibly the petals of a flower. I imagined the shadow sitting on my bench, tracing my footsteps, following me home. The shadow knew who I was and where I lived. Perhaps this shadow had followed me for a long time and today was the first day I became aware of my own vulnerability. I had never feared for my own life. Since Eliza's death, I viewed myself as a person who understood what violence was about, deciphered its secret codes, and gained through suffering an invulnerability to pain or danger. But today, along with my shield of unhappiness, that invulnerability melted. Today, I began to sense the shadow of doubt. I entered my room, closed the venetian blinds to block the fading sunlight, and turned on the light so that I could examine everything inside. I listened carefully, holding my breath with attention. Isabella was speaking on the phone.

Yes, she came home, but I think she is sleeping. Is this urgent? Do you want me to wake her up? Okay. Right away.

Isabella then knocked on the door, gently, as if not wishing to disturb me. May I come in, she asked.

My heart skipped a beat. I was almost certain. One of the many shadows in this world, the many dark and devouring shadows, wanted to pursue me, to catch me so that I would not, in turn, pursue shadows like him. I asked Isabella who was on the phone. She answered nervously that it was a police detective who wanted to speak to me about the death of an acquaintance.

I began to breathe normally again. It was not a shadow pursuing me, it was one of the blundering lights engaged in an aimless search for shadows.

I got up, went to the phone, and said hello.

The man immediately introduced himself and said that he was conducting an investigation regarding John Petri's death.

I asked him why.

Why what?

Why was he conducting an investigation?

Because the medical examiners thought that he might have died from unnatural causes, he explained.

Such as? I asked.

Such as poison.

I see, I answered calmly. So why are you calling me?

Because you were one of the few people who visited him and brought him food, he replied.

Are you saying that I poisoned him? I asked very calmly.

I'm saying that you might have, he replied equally nonplussed.

Because?

Because he killed your girlfriend.

So he knew. I was an obvious suspect. But that did not matter.

I answered with conviction that I didn't do it and that if they wanted to charge me with a crime the police should produce some kind of evidence, not just a motive.

The conversation moved back and forth for a few more minutes, switching rapidly between his exacting a confession and my guiltless denial of the crime. Then it ended abruptly.

He said that once he gathered the evidence he would come with a warrant for my arrest.

I said fine and goodbye. Frankly, I was not at all intimidated or impressed. Theirs was such an easy search: and these people think they are doing good work; that they have a difficult job! The real difficulty consists of finding suspects who have no motive to kill, who do it simply for their pleasure, who move nimbly from state to state. The real difficulty consists of finding suspects who wipe away the traces of their crimes, who change identities and names. So far, I'm just an ordinary woman who engaged in a simple act of vigilante justice. To become more slippery, I would have to become a hunter of shadows, a hunter like them.

At night, I didn't worry about him, the man who had threatened to arrest me that day. No, him I could evade; he was easy to contend with. Even if caught and tried, a jury might understand the motivations for my action.

I was much more concerned about the shadow who had followed my path and could be lurking in a corner of my room at that very moment. I looked at the glowing red light of my alarm clock: it was three in the morning. Then I continued my search. I turned on the lights and examined the entire room. I looked in the closet first, feeling the clothes with both hands as if I were checking for hidden weapons on real human bodies. I lingered around the necklines of my dresses and blouses, squeezing tight with all my force, wrapping the fingers of one hand around those of the other and hurting myself to practice how I might hurt another.

Then I got down on my hands and knees, with my eyes pinned on the open closet. I was not yet convinced that I had not been tricked. I looked carefully under the bed, gathering the dust in my hands, examining the proof that no one could have hid there for at least a few days. Next, I checked out the drawers of my desk, looked underneath the desk, and finally turned off the light and peered outside, through the narrow slits of the closed blinds. I had learned to peep through the blinds like a voyeur or criminal, looking through the tiny holes that interwove the string which held the blinds neatly together, in their regular horizontal rows. Examining the night through those tiny holes, I pretended to be a shadow woman ready to rip open men's bodies and lives. Then I took my flashlight and proceeded to examine all the other rooms, including Isabella's, as carefully as I had my own. I checked out the kitchen, opened the closet doors with a violent thrust, then flashed the light full blast to expose a possible intruder. I found nothing, but heard everything I needed to hear.

I heard the voice of my soul beckoning softly to my mournful heart, urging me like a sad prophecy to leave this empty house and fulfil my nightmare visions. I heard the news and the noise on t.v. shows and the man I had killed tell

me in multiple tongues that thousands and thousands more
women would die if I did not do something to stop it; if I did
not fling my body, night and day, between murderers and
victims. And I came to understand. I understood now that
Eliza's tragic death could serve a purpose. My worse fear was
alayed. She had not died in vain. Her death had transformed
me into a quiet and transparent medium of human justice.

Pleasure, mystery, fascination. Could I channel these
feelings to slightly different ends? I wondered. How nice it
would be if I could transform my sense of horror at the
sacrifice of women into a pleasure that would repel and
fascinate others. How nice it would be to experience a sense of
erotic excitement without any desire, arousal or seduction; a
thrill more powerful, solipsistic and direct than any consent
could possibly offer. I wish to sense a touch that leaves no
shared memories in its path. I wish to leave a trace made only
of droplets of blood, multiple wounds, castration, and a
grinning corpse as its signature style. As for the rest, the
audience watching me from afar, I would leave nothing up to
their imagination but the act itself. How was he abducted? By
whom? Did he know he was going to die? What did he feel or
think before and during his moment of death? Certainly,
killing men would be a mere mimicry or inversion of some
men's behavior toward some women. Nothing original or
complex; an act that could be easily perceived and
understood. But a surprising and spectacular act, nonetheless.

* * *

My ideas began to feel logical, lucid, coherent. It was
as if I had experienced a revelation. I felt that I had found a
partial solution, a sufficiently loud scream or protestation, to a
problem that had destroyed my life and the lives of other
women. Like all revelations, this one dissipated to the point
where the logic and sequence of its ideas seemed unclear as
soon as I thought I had grasped their clarity. Nevertheless, I
felt that indeterminate sense of lightness and relief that
accompanies any prophetic dream. It didn't matter to me that
I no longer knew what the dream meant, or if it meant
anything at all. What mattered was that the dream moved
through me in a way that resembled a process of thought,

worked me up to a resolve and changed me in a way that appeared exciting and significant.

I entered Isabella's room. Isabella woke up at the touch of my hand, shielded her half-open eyes from the light and asked me in a rough voice to turn off the t.v. or shut the door, since she was tired and trying to sleep. I told her that the tv had been off for hours. I was just talking to myself. Then I asked her to stop being abrupt and angry with me. I asked her to understand.

What is there to understand? she replied. Other than the fact that you are behaving so incomprehensively and that we have become complete strangers to each other? Her voice trailed off, whispering: I don't even know why we are still together... After a long pause, she added: People who knew you before, your own acquaintances, can no longer recognize you. She looked me straight in the eyes: Can you even recognize yourself, Joan?

Her question made me feel uncomfortable. I did not wish to be judged by people who could not even imagine what I was going through or what I had experienced. So I just answered dryly: I cannot bring myself to care about what other people think about me. I may care about what they think about life, or about each other. But not about me. I'm just an observer.

Isabella looked surprised.

What do you mean by that? Are you so full of yourself, do you consider yourself so far above us mere mortals, that you don't care about what we think about you or how you come across? Or do you think that you are so different from the rest of us that we don't see you at all; that you don't even cast a human shadow?

I haven't really thought about myself in any of those terms, I replied quite honestly. I don't consider myself as either in-human or super-human. In fact, I don't consider my humanity at all. Eliza's senseless death made me realize that I haven't yet understood what other people's humanity entails; what the codes of humanity urge us to be. So, I concluded, I can hardly tell where I stand with respect to those codes and practices.

It is very strange to hear you say this. It is even hypocritical, I would say. You were the one trying to prove the killer's inhumanity, or bad humanity, as you called it. You were the biggest humanist...

Not anymore, I interrupted.

Why not?

Because believing in humanity does not seem possible in this world. Before Eliza died, and even during the trial, I relied upon a conception of humanity that was at least somewhat other-regarding, non-arbitrary, based upon noble feelings. After the trial, after the verdict of not guilty, I could no longer believe in that myth.

I'm not sure why, Isabella considered the issue more calmly. Nobody said the killer behaved ethically. They just said he behaved like a man who is not in possession of his faculties, who is incapable of making good ethical decisions.

Yes I know. That is precisely why the trial made me viscerally disgusted and dizzy, dizzy from nausea and pain and the inability to see why that judgment was right or to explain why it was wrong; and, after all was said and done, to care about the difference between right and wrong.

Isabella looked skeptical. You sound like a moral relativist, she said, when, really, you are a moral absolutist in disguise. If everyone does not agree with your ethical views, if unanimity of judgment is not guaranteed, then you abandon moral reflection.

Yes. You are right. I have come to see the futility of debates when the world turns around so many competing and self-serving moral standards. It's not only consensus that is impossible, as you suggest, but also discussion and understanding. It is time that I stop trying to understand and begin to act.

Act how? Like an abnormal, weird person?

Isabella, I told you before that I don't care about what people think or say about me. I no longer measure myself up against the standards of humanity, of normality or of any particular identity at all. I have been too disappointed by those standards and the ways in which so many people violate them and get away with it. At the same time, it is true that I would prefer that other people did not evaluate or think about me either, since that would help me continue to suspend judgment about myself.

But don't you think that you should judge yourself a little more? retorted Isabella. Wouldn't it be nice if you thought more about how you come across to others or about the implications and effects of your actions?

No, not really. You see, if people's opinions did not affect me much at all, if I would manage to protect myself from their judgment, then I could do whatever I wished to do, go wherever my thoughts and inclinations would lead me.

I'm afraid to ask, but what is it that you wish to do? And what do you mean by your thoughts and inclinations leading you? Are you just a puppet moved by your drives or ideas?

It was just a figure of speech. I meant to say something more specific: I feel like I am starting to cope with Eliza's death in a more positive way.

Isabella shook her head in disagreement: No. As far as I can tell, you are more withdrawn and out of control than immediately after it happened.

Perhaps. I was too shocked at first to react in any way. I was emotionally paralyzed. But now I can react. I can do something about it.

What? What can you do? Resurrect her from the dead? Kill yourself? What?

No, I won't kill myself. And I know very well that I can't bring Eliza back to life. But I can make others aware of what she might have felt before her death and of how I feel now, without her. Don't worry. I don't plan to do anything unusual, I tried to reassure her. I just need some time alone to cope with my feelings. I want to take a few months off from school to work out my problems alone before burdening others with them.

Isabella failed to understand what I was saying. She simply answered: So, in other words, you are planning to leave me?

No, not for good. I just need to take the time alone to deal with my experience and emotions. I don't think that I can keep on living like this, trying and failing to pretend that nothing happened, being bottled up with anger and pain, bursting out inappropriately, feeling confused and abandoned. I have reached my limit and am about to explode.

Why must you explode? Why can't you cope with your pain like a normal person would, by talking about it, by seeking the support of family and friends, or by going for counseling?

Because all the talk about pain only amplifies its effects. The more I talk about what happened, the more angry I become. And yet I continue to think about it, to spin yarns of imaginary scenarios around it, to build my cocoon so that I can have a dwelling, the boundaries of a self to help me survive this nightmare that has become my life.

Isabella let out a torrent of remonstrative questions. Why do you torture yourself about what happened so much? Why can't you overcome your suffering and still continue to love Eliza for all that you have shared in the past and me for our present and future together? Why can't you allow us to lead a normal life? Why can't we build our happiness together, slowly and tenderly, without carrying around your burden of anguish, hatred and regret?

I thought that I saw tears condensing in Isabella's beautiful eyes. Perhaps I only imagined them. I looked at her, then looked aside, and felt that her questions couldn't be answered. All this anger and pain, there was no reason for nurturing it like a pleasurable wound, or spreading it around to the people I loved, or even to those I hated. It was just a disease, a contagious and incurable virus, that attacked each organism with whom I came into contact. And in each person I touched, it assumed a slightly different pattern and effect, generating a new violent strain for which there would be no solace or cure.

* * *

Looking into my own eyes, I could not recognize myself. Long blond hair, blue contacts, new style of clothes, and a suitcase. This was the new me. Each mirror and window I passed convinced me that I had left behind not only my life, but also my identity. Where was the small woman with brown eyes and short dark hair with whom I had grown familiar all my adult life? Where were the boyish clothes, the straight pants and loose sweaters, that had enfolded the body I could hardly recognize? Was it the same body? I stepped into a clothes store just to check: was I myself? Who was I? I pretended to try on a red dress, if only to convince myself of the continuity of my existence. Looking in the mirror, two milky blue eyes stared back at me in dismay. They were the eyes of a doll: empty of expression, of specks or other markings, of life. Wide open and beautiful. Were these eyes really mine? Could I express sadness, hatred, passion or love with them? I really couldn't tell.

I touched my long hair with equal unfamiliarity. It felt silky, soft and artificial. Long yellow strands slipped between my fingers, flowing back straight unto my shoulders. A shade of red lipstick shielded my lips from sight while making the lips of the new woman appear more visible. A pair of diamond earings glimmered among strands of hair. Eliza's earings. This was the only sign that my previous life was still flowing through me, through the same organs and veins of blood. Because externally, everything else had changed.

Would you like to try a different size ma'm? the salesclerck asked.

No thanks, I answered. I think that this color is too bright for me. When I stepped out of the fitting room, the saleslady looked skeptical. How could red be too bright for a woman who looked as tacky as myself? I was still holding on to my old sense of taste: that was a mistake. I looked at the salesclerk and told her I had changed my mind. The red dress went well with the red lipstick and blond hair. She agreed. I bought it and decided to avoid looking in mirrors. No matter how many different wigs, styles of clothes or colored contacts I would change. I had to get used to not having a stable look or shape. I had converted into a chameleon; into a being that changed colors, shed its skin, and hid beneath rocks. Getting used to this constant self-differentiation; to this life of no longer even trying to recognize myself, was the new challenge "we" had to face.

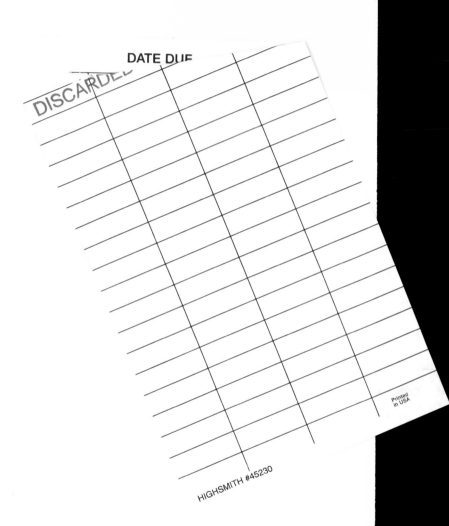